A MOUNTAIN
TOO HIGH

A MOUNTAIN TOO HIGH

THE TRUE STORY THAT INSPIRED THE MOTION PICTURE STAND YOUR GROUND

A NOVEL BY

MICHAEL MCCLENDON

BASED ON THE JOURNEY OF **JACKIE CARPENTER**

XULON **PRESS**

Xulon Press
2301 Lucien Way #415
Maitland, FL 32751
407.339.4217
www.xulonpress.com

Unless otherwise indicated, Scripture quotations taken from the King James Version (KJV)–public domain.

Printed in the United States of America.

ISBN-13: 9781545640494

TABLE OF CONTENTS

PROLOGUE

THE HOUSE WOULD CLING TO THE SIDE OF A WOODED HILL, AND overlook her mama and daddy's house.

She pulled the quilt back from her face and peered out at the workers already picking their way through the Tennessee Fieldstone which lay, waiting, at the construction site. Her house. Her dream house. Snuggled here in her parents' home, in the very bed which had cradled her as a little girl, she could not believe how blessed her life had become. Jackie Carpenter was living her girlhood dream.

Jackie crawled out of bed and put on a solid white jogging suit. This was best for visiting the site, as it made her look and feel like one of the painters. Jackie wanted to be a part of the building process, since she had designed the house herself, from the sprawling Mediterranean style, to the rock and iron gate that, reaching heavenward, would open onto the winding, pine-shadowed driveway. Her assistance at this stage usually consisted of keeping her dog Bojangles out of fresh cement, or helping her daddy steer around the massive worksite in his golf cart, but she loved being in the midst of it all. Far back as she could remember, this house had been in her head. Crazy! A house with a swimming pool in the living room! And all the rooms encircling the pool, with striped awnings and massive doors opening up to bring nature into the house. And yet, it was taking shape before her very eyes, a gift from Larry, her beloved husband of sixteen years, and a testament to the artistry of her youngest son, Jason. Jason was soon to enter the ministry, like his older brother Jim had done, and Jason intended to keep his construction business as well.

Settling into her parents' sunny kitchen, she cradled the mug of coffee her mother had just brewed. Soon she and mom would walk up the hill, with dad in his golf cart and assorted rescue dogs bouncing gleefully behind. Jackie wished Larry could be here to see the house taking shape, but he was back in their south Georgia home, running his business. "Maybe tomorrow," she thought. "Maybe he'll drive up tomorrow and surprise me".

Slats of morning sun were beginning to creep across the kitchen floor. Jackie's gaze once again was drawn up the hill. This was the land of her childhood. These same woods which had been witness to skinned knees, climbed trees, and summer campouts, would now part to allow her home to nestle within them. The little Georgia girl who had run these fields had now raised her children on these same acres and saw her sons raising their children as well. "Georgia land is good." Jackie murmured to the steam rising from her cup. "Georgia land gives you strong roots and stays in your blood. God has blessed this land. And me. And us."

Jackie's life was perfect. She had everything she wanted. In just a few hours, in the space of twelve minutes, everything would change. And in less than a year, Jackie Carpenter would die.

CHAPTER ONE

JASON'S HEAD WAS BURIED IN THE FRIDGE. WHEN HE HAD FINished his search, Jackie would quiz him about this visit. Jackie and Larry's south Georgia home was out of his way, to say the least, and she was needled by an uneasy curiosity surrounding his unannounced arrival.

"You used to do that when you were little."

Jason's head appeared briefly from behind the door. "What? Do what?"

"Stand in front of the refrigerator, just swinging the door back and forth, trying to decide what to eat."

"And you used to tell me to decide what I wanted *before* I opened the door, which makes absolutely no sense to me." He hefted a jug of sweet tea over one arm and attempted to take a swig.

"Now does Steph let you do that at home?" Jackie snapped as she took the jug from him and poured a glass, handing it to him along with a floral paper napkin.

"Stephanie can't tell me what to do; she's not my mother."

Jason had married a model-pretty young lady who had turned out to be even more beautiful inside. And they had given her a grandson: six year old J.J. Jackie couldn't help but smile at Jason's

1

comment. Here was her little boy again; feisty and funny. Curiosity getting her now, Jackie took the leap.

"So how did I rate this visit anyway?"

"I'm headed over to the new subdivision. Mom, they hit me again last night."

With this, her heart took a half-beat. Copper thieves had been assaulting Jason's new homes for months now. With the houses almost finished, the thieves would enter the empty complex in darkness and rip out copper pipes to sell on the black market. He was losing thousands of dollars which came out of his own pocket. There seemed no end to this.

"Again?! That same subdivision?"

Jason hopped up onto the kitchen counter and stared at his glass. "Yep. Same one. And each one they hit costs me about six thousand dollars."

"And why don't the police do something about it?"

"Mom, the police can't do anything with copper thieves unless they catch them in the act. And they don't have the manpower to keep an officer on the site, so.....so, I'm going to spend the night out there and watch."

Jackie felt cold. She turned away and looked out into the sunshine, but shivered anyway.

"Jason, please tell me you are not serious."

"Now get that look off your face - you and Steph! - all I have to do is hide and watch and if anybody comes up, I'll just call the police. They said they'd have an officer patrolling the area and come right over. Mom, I have to. It's secluded out there and they'll just keep coming back. I'm going to hire a night watchman, but Monday's the soonest they can start."

Considering turning up the thermostat, Jackie just stood stock still instead. It occurred to her that the chill she was feeling had nothing to do with the room temperature.

"Mom, I'll just watch." An impish smile played around Jason's mouth. "Nothing's gonna happen to me."

This particular site was way off the main road. Completely cut off. Secluded and dark. "Well, I'm gonna say a prayer for you just in case. So you won't be alone out there."

Jackie was sitting at her wooden desk. The school bell was ringing; it seemed as if it had been ringing for a long time. All of her classmates rose, silently, and left the room. Her teacher gave her an odd look and exited as well. Still Jackie remained seated, all alone. And the bell rang and rang.

"I got it, I got it, " Larry mumbled in the half light. Jackie realized her hand was grasping for the insistently ringing phone on his side of the bed.

The bedside lamp blinded Jackie, but at least the ringing had stopped. Larry cleared his throat and spoke. "He-hello?"

"Why did they all leave me alone in the classroom?" Jackie thought. "Why isn't Larry saying anything? Am I still dreaming?" She rolled over and focused on the bedside clock. Two-twenty in the morning.

Larry barked at the mouthpiece, uncustomarily stern, "Just say it." Then after a pause, "Oh, no."

Jackie ripped the phone from Larry's hand and pressed it to her ear. Someone was speaking but she couldn't make sense of the fragments, "...can't stop the bleeding...Jason and Billy...police got there too late..."

Jackie threw herself to the floor, a tangle of sheets and phone cord and arms. Why was Larry holding her? She had to get to Jason! The more she struggled, the harder he attempted to restrain her.

"You can't see him. Jackie! They won't let you see him! We have to stay here and wait. Jackie!"

She stopped struggling, looked into her husband's eyes and tried to understand what he was telling her.

"Wait?" She was aghast at how absurdly inappropriate this idea was. "Wait?! Wait. Oh, Dear Lord. I have to wait."

Contentious birds scuttered and fluttered on the lawn. Jackie sat, fully dressed, on the veranda outside the bedroom. In one hand she held her purse, fingers pressed deep into the soft leather, and in the other she gripped the cordless phone to her bosom. Morning was beginning to reveal a silhouette of the treeline in the distance, but Jackie did not see the dawn.

"Ms. Jackie. He's dead." It was Stephanie's voice on the phone, but Jackie could not remember the ring, or answering it.

Stephanie seemed to be struggling to form words; her voice sounded heavy and forced. "That man - that man - he died and they're saying, they're saying that Jason, and my daddy, they're saying -- "

Jackie heard Stephanie stifle a cry, but from a distance, and another voice came onto the line.

"Jackie? Jackie, this is Ellis. I've got some things to say to you and Larry, but I don't want to say it over the phone. Jackie?"

Suddenly on her feet, she addressed Ellis with a commanding fury that stunned him.

"Ellis, you talk to me *right now*, do you hear me?"

"Do you want to see Jason?"

This statement cut through to her and left her silent.

"All right then. Is Larry good to drive?"

The Carpenter's SUV was sliding along a tree-lined Georgia highway. Larry looked straight ahead and managed to drive the speed limit, but not one mile over. Jackie was holding the dashboard with one hand, her Bible in the other. They drove on.

"You want music?"

Jackie gripped the Bible tighter. Larry tried again. "Baby, you want music? You want some music on?" Still nothing. "Honey, Ellis knows what to do."

"No."

"No he don't know?"

"No music."

"Oh. Okay."

"He don't either."

"Don't what?"

"He don't know. What to do."

"Ellis?"

"He's just Jason's real estate attorney, Larry. He closes on houses. He can't help."

"He's a good man, though. Smart."

"Yes."

"Yes, smart?"

"Music."

Larry leaned forward and turned on the radio. A gentle praise song filled the air. Heavy tears began to slide down Jackie's face. "Larry, I haven't prayed."

"You haven't prayed? When, when haven't you prayed?"

"Never, not since this whole thing happened last night,"

"Jackie, the first thing out of your mouth was, 'Oh, Lord.'"

"I've called His name, but I have not prayed. I been busy trying to handle all this myself. But I need to ask Him to take care of it. Cause I can't."

Larry slid his hand over near hers. She released her grip on the dash and took it. And together they sped down the highway toward Jason.

CHAPTER TWO

AFTER A FRANTIC SEARCH FOR A PARKING SPACE, JACKIE AND Larry made their way through the construction cones and concrete dust into the brand new courthouse No one, not even the bewildered government workers inside, could tell them where to go. Charging up and down the echoing halls, they finally spotted a familiar figure. Tucked beside a gleaming staircase, Ellis stood holding Stephanie's hand. With his short-cut salt and pepper hair, Ellis looked more like a high school athletic coach than an attorney. His tennis shoes and windbreaker gave him an even more boyish appearance as he turned and waved at the pair bolting toward him. "He's so small," Jackie thought distractedly, "how can he possibly help us?"

"Where is he; when can I see him?!" Jackie's voice echoed off the halls and pulled curious faces her way. "Where is--"

Ellis cut her off. "Now, y'all just be still and let me catch you up. Stephanie, your daddy came and woke me up this morning and told me what happened. I went right over to the judge's office, but the deputy – he's the one who gave Jason advice on guarding the site – had got to the judge first. This Deputy Book told the judge that Jason was in a rage about the copper thefts and his intentions were to kill somebody—"

"He did *what?*"

"Honey!" Larry held up a hand to silence Jackie. His other hand was supporting Stephanie, who was half-slumped against him.

"I know," Ellis pushed on, "but because the deputy has made these accusations, the judge has no choice but to charge Jason with felony murder."

"This can't be happening," Jackie prayed aloud.

"Larry, Stephanie, Jackie; hold it together now. For Jason. He's gonna need you all. You have fifteen minutes with him at 1 o'clock. Let's get over to Cell Block A."

Seated on cheap metal chairs, Jackie and Larry and Stephanie waited in the county jail holding room. The linoleum floor, perhaps white in its youth, was now a sick yellow, layered with suspicious stains, spots, and cracks. The fluorescent lights buzzed and flickered overhead and cast an unnatural light down on the packed room. All around them, people leaned, dozed, fought, or just gazed off in defeat or disinterest. A few sat on the floor. Jackie stared at the toenails of the grimy woman in front of her. She wondered why such a person would wear sandals in public. She wondered why the tough-looking kid in the corner was sobbing into his cell phone. She wondered why she was here, and in an absurdly comic moment, thought she might just rise, straighten her dress, and walk out the door. *Clang!* There it was again, that sound of heavy metal doors being slammed shut. And voices in the distance, shouting and begging, and threatening and cussing. *Clang!* Jackie shivered.

"I don't think...." Stephanie trailed off.

Jackie was suddenly aware that Ellis was standing beside them, leaning against the green cinderblock wall. "What is it, Stephanie?"

"I don't think I...," she continued, "...don't think I can do this don't think I can...."

A woman in a leg cast began to shriek with laughter. Ellis moved in protectively on his friends.

"Don't even think about yourself. Just think about Jason and how you can help him."

"Will they let us touch him?" Jackie spoke up.

"No, he'll be back behind a partition. And chances are he'll look bad--"

"Bad *how*" Jackie demanded.

"Well, he'll be shackled and likely he'll be wearing the red jumpsuit; red for murder--"

Stephanie echoed, "Murder."

"Those are the charges; that's just how the system works," Ellis continued his explanations, "but mostly he'll look bad because of the trauma. Emotional trauma is just as powerful as physical trauma, so be prepared. And remember this: He's inside and can't do a thing. Don't put anything on him; he's helpless. Jason's depending--."

Clang! This time the sound was much closer and a strapping prison guard with a shaved head abruptly appeared behind Ellis.

"Anyone headed to Cell Block A, step this way." Because those holding the large plastic cards were not moving fast enough to suit the guard, he raised his voice. "If you are holding a red card with an A on it, stand up and follow me."

And they were moving. A few others from the waiting area were with them; Ellis was left behind. As they walked the halls, the sounds and smells, only hinted at earlier, moved in on them. An inmate shouted at them from a room filled with shelves of towels and sheets, while others moved back as they passed, pulling their mops and brooms close and lowering their eyes. Guards moved about. Doors clanged. And they walked. Suddenly they had been herded into a tiny area which reminded Jackie of old fashioned phone booths; just a little space with a tiny, worn seat and a battered black phone. Bodies were pressed all around. Jackie pushed Stephanie into a seat and hovered close. Larry pressed back against the wall, attempting in vain to give them some space. The door was shut upon the family and the dozen or so strangers who accompanied them. "Trapped," Jackie thought. "We're all in prison and can't get out until someone else decides to let us go."

The heavy door glimpsed through the Plexiglas partition burst open and inmates began to file in. They were all dressed in red, just as Ellis had predicted, and they each appeared to be dirty or sick or dangerous or unsavory in some manner. One was Jason.

"I didn't mean to hurt anybody. It was an accident; I wish I hadn't even gone down there!" Jason was just inches away, crying like he was just a little boy, and his mama could not even touch him. Jackie felt she might literally die. She felt she might physically punch through the milky Plexiglas and lift him in her arms and run away. But then she saw and heard herself, as she lifted the phone from its grimy holder. "Pick up your phone; Jason, pick up the phone." Jason had not lifted the receiver and Jackie had been merely reading his lips. Jackie placed her hand flat on the glass and looked directly at Jason, demanding he look at her. Uncertainly, he lifted the phone to his ear. "Jason, you listen to me, ya hear? Listen to your mama. Hey, Bird, you remember when you told me you were going to spend the night down at the site and I said I was going to say a prayer for you just in case? Well, that means you weren't alone out there and you are not alone in here now. You will get through this but you have to stay strong. Now, soon as we leave here we'll go get you out on bond. Okay? Okay?"

Jason finally looked into his mother's eyes and lifted his hand, pressing it to hers through the glass. "'kay."

She placed the phone firmly into Stephanie's hand. "Talk to him. Talk to him, Stephanie."

Both husband and wife were sobbing and snuffling like little children, but finally managed to speak.

"Hi, Honey."

"How are you, Steph? How's J.J.?"

"Oh, he's fine. He's...he's just confused."

"What did you tell him?"

"Oh, not much, I--"

"Steph, Stephanie, put the phone back up to your mouth; I can't hear--"

"I didn't tell him much, cause I....but I'll have to tell him something soon."

"Don't tell him....don't tell..." Jason crumbled and sobbed.

"Jason, look at me; don't you hide your face from me, you look at me!"

"I can't I--"

"Look at me, Jason! You have to come home, do you hear me? You have to come home to us. Jason...look at me..."

Laughter broke out from the stall next to them. Suddenly Jackie was aware of all the voices around her, crossing and blending; cries and words and pleas, all rising and blurring together. She could no longer pick out which was Jason's.

11

CHAPTER THREE

LARRY'S BALLGAME WAS A DULL ROAR ON TV AND BOJANGLES whimpered and whined at Jackie as she paced the living room carpet, cordless phone at her ear.

Even with the mightiest of efforts, they had not been able to get Jason out on bond, but at least Monday would be his preliminary hearing. Yes, tomorrow, the judge would hear the absurd accusations and send him home. Even if he had to face some minor charges later on, he would be safely out of that place. What was happening to him, even now? She just wanted to talk to him and reassure him. Jackie turned her attention back to the singularly hateful woman on the other end of the line.

"Yes, ma'am, yes, I do understand that, but they told us we could see him in person once a week and-- It's just that we haven't been able to---"

Pacing, she managed to step on Bojangles paw and he emitted an unearthly shriek.

"Yes, but the preliminary hearing is tomorrow and we just need to speak--"

Larry stuck his head in the door and offered, "Ellis said we need to get Jason one of those PayPal cards so he can call us--"

The ballgame droned on.

"It's urgent that we speak to him and we have no way--"

"And then he can call us whenever he wants..." Larry continued.

A perky jingle spit from the television set, alerting the world to a new weight-loss program. The phone's second line began to ring insistently.

"--I have another call and I – ma'am? –ma'am, I just hope you never find yourself on my end of a call like this one. Bojangles! Sit, now, sit! Yes, hello? Stephanie. What? Today? Larry, did you get the Sunday paper yet?"

"Naw, not yet; it's still out on the--"

"Well, go get it - now! Stephanie, how can they say that? Go get it, Larry! They can't just say things like that—Stephanie, somebody's beeping in again. Bo, sit! Hold, on, Honey; you all just hold on---hel-hello? Mama? Well, what is it? Just say it."

Larry returned from the porch, rolling the red rubber band down the newspaper. "They don't put these in plastic anymore?"

"Larry, Mama says turn the TV on channel 32. *Now*, Larry, hurry; Mama says something's on 32 right now."

Pushing through the channels, Larry settled on a news report. The house in the background looked familiar. It was one of Jason's houses; the house where Jason waited for the copper thieves. But now it was criss-crossed with yellow crime scene tape, and black-booted workers milled about, their orange jackets seeming to glow in the gloom. A dirty white van sat in the gravel drive. And there, standing beside a dark, muscular police officer, and two people Larry and Jackie did not recognize, was local reporter DeAundria Keana Kelly. Suddenly, with an exaggerated attitude of outrage, she spoke.

"--standing on the very spot where, just over 24 hours ago, these two men saw their cousin gunned down in cold blood. Mr. Morales, can you tell us, in a few words, what happened on the night of February 29?"

A young man with dark skin, curly hair, and a goatee began to speak in a thick accent, as DeAundria shoved the microphone to his mouth. Despite her attempt to aim him at the camera, he continued to reel off his words directly to her, and in a rapid manner.

"We left to eat and then we came back to sleep here so we could get to work on the house early in the morning. Then when we were going to sleep a man with a flashlight knocked on the van and told us to get out and then he walked up behind my cousin and shot him. He killed my cousin with his gun."

DeAundria wheeled to the camera with a look of triumph on her face. "And the questions continue in this shocked community, as one shattered family searches for answers to this vicious and unprovoked attack. This is DeAundria Keana Kelly; WOCF, Channel 32." Then breaking into a broad smile, "Channel 32 and *you*!"

And, without warning, the screen was filled with women riding on their shopping carts and dancing down a supermarket aisle. The music blared from the screen, as Jackie suddenly felt the phone in her hand begin to ring. Or was that the doorbell? It was both. The phone was ringing and someone was at the door. Jackie stared at her cell phone, which had just begun to vibrate its way across the coffee table. The doorbell was joined by a steady, demanding knock. The phones rang and the bells rang and Bojangles began to bark and bark and bark at whoever was knocking at the door as Jackie stood perfectly still in her perfect living room. The paper in Larry's hand fell to the floor, revealing the headline, LOCAL BUILDER

CHARGED IN VICIOUS MURDER. Jackie stood and Bojangles barked and the shoppers on television just kept on singing.

When she awoke in darkness with her heart pounding, she did not know where she was, or why she should be so completely filled with dread. Finally, hearing familiar voices coming from a distance, she remembered: She and Larry had spent the night at her mama and daddy's house, so they would have a shorter drive to the courthouse. Today was Jason's preliminary hearing. Jackie knew she should be filled with hope - Jason would be released from jail today - but the weight of courtrooms and uniforms and seeing her son put on public display forced her to clench her eyes shut and try to return to the heavy blanket of sleep. The last time she slept in this bed, she had arisen to stroll about the work site on the hill, watching her new home take shape. Now the abandoned site could only remind her of how many dreams had been smashed on the night of February 29.

Even before the soft knock on the bedroom door, Jackie smelled her mama's rich coffee.

"Jackie? Sweetie? Time ya'll got up now."

Jackie turned gently in bed, so as not to disturb Larry. She found the bed empty. He must already be up. Jackie's mama sat carefully on the edge of the bed, cradled the coffee in her daughter's hand, then reached to softly push the hair back off Jackie's forehead. Just like when she was a girl.

"You need to get up now, Sweetie, and face the day."

"Mama, how do I?"

"How do you what?"

"How do I get up out of this bed?"

"Now, how can you ask me that?"

Jackie managed a swallow of coffee. "What you mean, Mama?"

"Cause you know the answer to that one. You get up out of the bed, like you do anything else that hurts or scares you. You do it for folks you love. You do it for your babies. Now get up."

Jackie looked at her mama's face in the amber light filtering in from the hall. For just a moment, her face looked soft and youthful again. Abruptly, Jackie was aware of movement outside her windows. Engine sounds, lights moving through the curtains, then distant voices made their way from the hill.

"Mama, what's - who's that?"

"Oh, it's them workers on the house. I guess they're starting early this morning."

"But, Jason's....but, workers?

"Aw, yeah, Jim came out and told them what happened and some walked off, knowing they probly wasn't going to get paid. But some stayed. And come back the next day, too. More'n half of Jason's workers been back every single day. One of 'em tole me they want Jason to be proud of the work they done for you when he comes back home."

And Jackie's mama held her little girl and let her cry and cry. Then, together, they arose and headed for court.

They had been sitting in an airless jury deliberation room for a very long time. Jackie read her Bible and tried not to let her mind wander. It had been hours since they heard any footsteps clack down the hall. Jackie wondered if having a clock on the wall would help or just make things worse. The ticking would help. Or maybe it wouldn't. Focus. Read your Bible.

Larry appeared to be studying the wall.

Suddenly Stephanie blurted, "How much longer do you think--"

17

"Jason musta been happy to get back into his own clothes." Jackie's voice seemed unnaturally loud.

Larry studied the wall. "Sure wish they had a window in this place."

Feeling she might have sounded too short with Stephanie, Jackie asked, "Did you bring his black suit?"

"Dark grey. What if he--"

"Wait till we get him out of here, Stephanie. Let's not talk about....Jim, what's your sermon gonna be about on Sunday?"

"It's from Matthew, Mom. ...*and sendeth rain upon the just and on the unjust.*"

"TV was callin' for rain," Larry offered.

"Maybe I shoulda brought his black."

"Thirty percent chance, so they said."

"Stephanie, grey's fine."

"Grey skies?"

"Suit."

"Black?"

"Grey."

The door opened silently and a steely woman stood just outside. Jackie noticed her hair was pulled so tight that the skin at the hairline was bloodless white.

"Follah me. Single file. Once we enter the courtroom, sit on the left-hand side. Immediate family members sit on the front row. And no tawkin'."

Jackie closed her Bible and placed it in her purse, then took Larry's hand. The little band followed the grey woman down nondescript hallways. There seemed to be no sound until a beefy guard opened the wooden double doors into the courtroom. The entire space seemed alive with noise and movement. The right side of the room was filled with observers and members of the media. Some relatives were already seated on the second bench to the far left, and near the front, Jason was seated, along with Ellis, at a small table. Jason, wearing his grey suit, turned and smiled at his family as they were seated on the front row. And on the right front of the courtroom, mirroring Jason's table, sat two people unknown to the family. The girl was very pretty and wore a pastel suit and a soft hairstyle that gently accentuated her perfect cheekbones. The young man could have been a model. Silence.

"All rise for the Honorable Judge Henry Strickland, Superior Court of the State of Georgia, Crockett Judicial Circuit."

The judge appeared to be a relaxed, grandfatherly sort. He sauntered to his seat and smiled warmly at the two fashion models seated before him, then glanced out at the remainder of the room.

"Ya'll sit down now and make yourselves comfortable." Oddly, Jackie found herself feeling a touch better. "Now before we begin this Preliminary Hearing, there are a few issues I'd like to address. First of all, to the members of the press: there are to be no television cameras..."

It seemed as if the judge would never stop laying out the rules, regulations, and parameters. So much of it meant nothing to the anxious family seated before him. And then he began to read files, documents, and a particularly outrageous written testimony from Deputy Clayton Book. Over the next several hours it was revealed that the pretty girl was Evelyn Pitt, the prosecuting attorney, and her model companion was the lead investigator in the case, a detective named Gus Crutcher. Both Ms. Pitt and Ellis questioned the detective. Testimonies of the dead man's two companions, Morales and Lerma, were read, and they were so conflicted and full of out-right contradictions that some passages even brought laughter from the observers.

Jackie could hardly contain herself. She just wanted to stand and address the judge, explain it was all a terrible mistake, and take Jason home.

Then, at last, the judge peered over his half-glasses at the court-room and began to speak.

"Having taken into account the written testimony of witnesses Mr. Morales and Mr. Lerma, and the written report of Crockett County Sheriff's Deputy Clayton Book, and in light of the cross-ex-amination of Detective Gus Crutcher by both you, Mr. Pitt, and you, Mr. Burdette, I find that the charge of felony murder will stand. Remove the defendant."

And so it was. Guards surrounded Jason and hoisted him to his feet. As they tried to force him to move faster, Jackie noticed Jason's ankles had been shackled all along, and the cuffs of his grey suit rested upon them. Jason tried to keep up with the guards, but was dragged each time he missed a step. He twisted his head one last time in an attempt to see his family, then was gone.

Jackie did not remember leaving the courtroom at all. She was not aware, even though she was later told, that Stephanie had fainted in the hallway and Jackie just walked around her. She knew nothing until Larry pulled to a stop in the parking lot and turned off the engine. She looked around at the shoppers strolling about the stores in the tiny strip mall.

"Larry, why are you - don't stop."

"I need charcoal."

"Go home. Take me home."

"Charcoal. And vinegar. I need vinegar and charcoal."

"Larry, I don't -- I'm not --"

"Friday. It's your birthday. I need charcoal. For the barbecue. And vinegar for my hot sauce. Everybody loves my hot sauce."

Jackie looked directly at Larry for the first time in a long while. He was sitting, quiet and solitary, looking out the windshield.

"No, Larry. No, Baby, not this year. Nobody will be expecting you to. No charcoal. No birthday picnic."

"I need to get the charcoal. And make my hot sauce. It's what I do."

As Larry walked across the parking lot to the store, he seemed very small. And he did not change his measured gait, even when it began to rain.

CHAPTER FOUR

THE SICKLY GREEN MASS COWERED ON THE PLATE, SHIVERING with indecision. To Jackie, it seemed for a moment as if it would leap back into the dessert mold and, in embarrassment, beg to be returned to the darkness of the refrigerator. Deep in the murky lime depths, small torpedo-like objects were suspended. Jackie wiped her hands on one of the Barnyard Shenanigans dish-towels that Stephanie's mom had given her last Christmas and gazed out her kitchen window. There, past the redwood deck, the smoke from the grill was beginning to nudge the balloons and streamers which had been hung in honor of Jackie's birthday. Her annual birthday barbecue. And the only birthday wish she had would not come true. There was no doubt she must face the festivities and all the guests who were waiting for her in the back yard. She had stalled as long as she could. Giving the countertop one last swipe with the towel, she hoisted the Jell-O mold and walked toward the back door, passing the laundry room on her right.

"Jason? Hi, Jason."

Jackie froze as her face grew hot and her hands icy at the sound of his name. "Jason?! Where was he? Here?!"

From the corner of her eye, she spied a familiar form, standing in the shadows of the laundry room. Silhouetted by the slats of pale light coming through the back window, stood her son.

"I...I don't know when you'll hear this, Jason," Jim began, "I know they took your cell phone. It's probably in a box somewhere with the rest of your things. So I don't know when you'll get this message. But I just wanted to call and hear your voice and..."

Jackie couldn't breathe and she could not move from this spot in the door frame. The dessert mold in her hand was perfectly still.

"It's Mom's birthday and we're having the barbecue like always...and we're having all your favorite food. I can't eat it. I tried. I'll wait until you can eat it with me. I guess I -- I don't know -- just wanted to say I miss my little brother --"

Abruptly, Jim ceased to speak and froze. After a moment, he began to lower the receiver, stopped, then brought it back to his ear again. Finally, he gently replaced the phone in its cradle. Shoving his hands in his back pockets, Jim lowered his head and his shoulders began to heave, though he made no sound.

Jackie burst through the back door and out into the bright March sunshine. She lurched halfway across the deck and stood, stunned and confused. Surely she was not supposed to continue. Surely there was some mistake in thinking she had to move, converse, function.

"Hey, Cousin, how you holdin' up?"

Jackie's cousin lifted herself off the green and yellow patio furniture and jogged over to greet her. Debbie was slightly older than Jackie, but filled with such life and energy that she could have been ten years her junior. Debbie's blond hair haloed her head, as befitting an angel. Resting her hand comfortably on Jackie's shoulder, she spied the dessert in Jackie's hands.

"Is that Wilma Jean's Jell-O mold? What's she put in there this time, pork rinds? I heard she puts turkey in it for Thanksgiving."

Jackie stared at the horizon. Debbie, unfazed, examined the green goo with exaggerated interest.

"Hmmmmm. Skittles? No. Boogers? Could be. Hey, you better laugh; you know I'm just gonna keep this up 'til you do."

Jackie's gaze drifted toward Debbie, and she smiled wanly, seeming to see her for the first time. Debbie drew her cousin gently toward the big patio umbrella and seated her on a comfy bench. A group of kids ran by, laughing and shouting. Debbie sat and looked around at the deck, the bright sky, and the distant tree line, starting to show a hint of green.

"We sure got a pretty day for the barbecue. Warm!"

"Debbie...I don't think this was such a good idea."

"Just look around at all these people in your back yard. There's that rowdy little Hinkle boy -- don't he come over after school and take Bojangles for a walk for you? And I know Dr. Massey calls and checks on you every day -- oh, man, I wish somebody would tell him that plaid shorts and varicose veins don't go together!"

Debbie reared back and cackled with laughter. Jackie stared impassively, but Debbie continued unfazed.

"You know what Cynthia's been doin' of the evenings? Building a prayer chain! She's called people from Georgia to New York and there are thousands of people praying for Jason; people we don't even know and don't know him. Isn't that a miracle? Honey, there's angels all around you; just look! Satan's having his butt kicked and I think that's a good enough reason to celebrate with potato salad and green Jell-O. But if it gets to be too much for ya, just lean your head on His shoulder and say, 'I'm tired.' I think He likes it when we come to Him like little kids."

Jackie leaned toward Debbie and rested her head against her cousin's.

"Hey! Remember when we were kids and we used to sit in those hard little yellow chairs in Sunday School? What was that song you and me used to sing at Sunbeams? *Little ones to Him belong. They are weak* -- C'mon, you remember -- *but He is strong...*"

Almost inaudibly at first, Jackie joined her cousin in the song.

"*Yes, Jesus loves me. Yes, Jesus loves me. Yes, Jesus loves me. The Bible tells me so.*"

And so they sat, two little girls in Sunday School, listening to the sound of a tinkly piano playing hymns for them. The sunshine bathed Jackie and warmed her hands. She felt comfortable, drowsy, and safe for the first time in....how long had it been? It didn't matter. Jesus loved her. And her family. And with Him all things are possible. And He has not given us a spirit of fear. She began to drift.

Debbie's easy voice brought her back to the sunny deck.

"You know what else Jesus is telling me? That if we don't get up off this chair right now, there ain't gonna be a single spare rib left on that grill!"

In spite of herself, Jackie began to laugh as Debbie grabbed an arm and hoisted her to her feet. Arms around each other's waists, they began to walk together toward the bellowing grill, where Larry, sporting a new "Boss of the Sauce" apron, was slathering his hot sauce on ribs and burgers. Abruptly, Debbie broke away and dashed back to retrieve Wilma Jean's Jell-O mold. Holding it up to the sunlight and examining its interior, she was finally able to make out what was captured firmly inside. Debbie shook her head and murmured in disbelief.

"Pinto beans."

Jason waited, almost naked, under unforgiving bare light bulbs. The inmates stood against cracked and stained tile, crawling with black mold, waiting for their weekly shower. The constant noise was almost unbearable in these close quarters. Everyone seemed to be shouting, screaming, and pounding and slapping with fists and hands. It never stopped. For no reason, Jason remembered today was his mom's birthday. That world seemed so far away. Would he ever see it again?

The men all wore their underwear into the shower. This should have given Jason some sense of comfort and modesty, but it did not. He remembered the words of his scrawny cellmate. "Don't *never* take off your skivvies; don't *never* take off your underwear. 'Til you're back in your cell and them doors are shut, you don't never show yerself nekkid in here."

A huge man with tattoos bumped up against Jason. Again. And again, but this time he stayed pressed against him. Jason was shaking uncontrollably and purple lips were barely covering his chattering teeth. He could feel the huge man's breath; he could smell it.

Suddenly a voice barked and Jason was shoved into the shower. No steam. No soap. Icy needles of water assaulted screeching bodies, and cries echoed off the chamber walls. Noise; always noise.

Jason's fragile cellmate stood beneath a shower just a few feet away. Without warning, a hulking brute and his two cohorts were on him. One flipped a towel over his face and pulled him backwards, blind and muted by the fabric. From that point, Jason could only see body parts, flailing arms, and the little guy's desperate attempts to free himself. Jason took one step forward but was punched and shoved back into the corner. He heard a muffled "Officer! Officer!" and took up the cry himself. Soon their voices were buried beneath cheers and whoops.

With one mighty lift, the biggest of the inmates hoisted the other boy's tiny frame almost over his head and tossed him into the far corner of the showers. And then they were on him. Jason slid down the cold tile wall in slow motion. Almost in the fetal position, he wanted to disappear. But instead, he just sat beneath the pin pricks of water and shook and stared.

"You have to get me out of here have to get me out have to get me out! I can't stay here another night I have to get out. Tell Larry to talk to Ellis. I don't belong here I'll never make it get me out!" Jason was attempting to be heard over the din of the prison community room but could not afford to let anyone see or hear his panic. This leant him the sound of a drowning man. All around him was the incessant noise and physical contact. Jason's hair was still wet from the shower. His skinny cellmate was nowhere to be seen.

Jackie's voice was deceptively calm. She seemed to be listening to herself speak from some distance, and she was hearing her words at the same time as Jason.

"Jason, listen to me – stop! You just listen to me and do exactly what I say. Jason, soon as you hang up, I want you to get a piece of paper and a pencil and I want you to draw the jail cell. Everything that you can see, I want you to draw it. Then I want you to write down everything that you need, and that you don't have. Now will you do that? Go on, Bird. That's your job now."

This seemed illogical, even as she heard herself say it, but it must have been one of those miracle moments when a mother's instincts took over and led her to perfectly tend to her child. Jason seemed to calm down.

"Okay, Mom. I'll do it. I'll draw."

"All right, then. You go get busy and I'll call Ellis right now."

"Bye, Mom."

"Bye, Bird."

Larry used to call Jason "Yardbird" when he was younger. Somehow that stuck and was shortened to Bird. Jackie always thought that fit him; he was destined to fly high. Her own little Bird. When Larry came into their lives, he became the boys' true and real father. They retained the Veitch name legally, but deep down they were Carpenters. They were Larry's boys and they loved him without reservation.

And now her Bird was in prison. Worse, he was in Cell Block A, which Ellis had admitted contained the "worst of the worst"; the most dangerous and deadly criminals in the system.

Suddenly Jackie heard Ellis' voice on the phone, and she burst forth with fury. She could not recall dialing him.

"Ellis, you get him out! Get him out now! You have to do something, he is dying in there; he can't take it another second. You have to do something now!"

Ellis sounded bored. No, tired. "Jackie, how many times do I have to tell you this? Until his bond hearing, there is nothing you can do. Nothing."

The calm that Jackie had heard earlier in her own voice now seemed to suffuse her entire being. She, for the first time in weeks, knew exactly what to do. Pulling a long coat over her jogging outfit, she passed through the front door and watched the front steps slip under her feet. She was in the car and it was gliding down the drive, the sound of screeching tires coming from far away. The drive down was easy and soft; she felt as if she was cradled in cotton, and all the lights changed to let her big black car pass through them. Outside Jim's church, she pulled to a stop and mounted the stairs without bothering to turn off the engine or close the car door. One hand held flat in front of her caused the big front door to open and it banged, soundlessly it seemed, against the wall as she passed. Jackie felt she was coasting down the aisle, much as she had coasted down Hulsey Hill on her bike when she was little. The sun cast a stained glass tint upon the very air and dust mites danced about her. She stopped just before the pulpit and looked up directly at the crucifix.

Jackie spoke honestly and directly from her heart. It was not a prayer. It was a mother's statement.

"My Dear Heavenly Father. You so loved the world that You gave us Your Only Begotten Son. But I cannot give mine. And I can't sit back and do nothing. If You are not going to fix this, then I will. I will. I will find a way. If You won't, then I will."

Jackie turned and went home. Determined.

Jason was making a list to the side of his pencil drawing of the jail cell, just like his mother had asked: 9) no windows, 10) no pillow, 11) no salt, 12), no pepper, 13) no privacy, 14) no dignity....he glanced up at the big institutional clock across the block. Five minutes till 6. Jason placed his drawing beside his cot, on top of all the other drawings. How many would more would there be? He stood and placed his hands on the cold iron bars, watching the minute hand jump, jump, jump. Four minutes till six. Please. Please. It's almost six.

Stephanie sat on her piano bench, watching the hands on the tiny gold and crystal clock. Three minutes after six. Please. It's after six. The phone rang only once before she had it to her ear. She strained to listen. "Okay, then," she thought, "if that's what we have, then that's what we get." She then reassured Jason. "Yes, my Sweet Boy. All right, then. Just as long as you can. Listen." And placing the receiver carefully on top of the piano, she began to play.

The noise in the block was penetrating. And yet Jason could hear every note that Stephanie was playing for him. He could almost see her, sitting at her beloved piano, her beautiful eyes looking at some distant view, her fingers flying over the keys as her voice lifted effortlessly.

I come to the garden alone, while the dew is still on the roses.

And the voice I hear, falling on my ear, the Son of God discloses.

The sounds of the prison were fading and Jason was hardly aware of them. He was in his own living room with his family. As Steph began the refrain, little J.J.'s reedy voice joined his mom's.

And He walks with me and He talks with me. And He tells me I am his own.

And the joy we share, as we tarry there, none other has ever known.

There was no sound around him. Only the music of his wife and child; clear, unassailable. He was there with them. He was home.

Stephanie, finishing the final chord, allowed her hand to linger on the last key. She did not move for a moment. Then she slowly reached for the telephone and lifted it to her ear. Nothing but the buzz of a disconnected phone. She put the phone back in its cradle. J.J. looked up at his mother expectantly. She took his pale hand in hers and the two of them sat at the piano, watching the sunlight fade from the hands on the little crystal clock.

The big man with the muscles was back. This guy was huge, hulking, and had a dead look in his pale eyes. He was one of the men who sent Jason's cellmate to the infirmary. And wherever Jason was, he seemed to be. Now, as Jason sat in his cell on this cold March day, he stood outside the bars, just watching. He had done that before. But this time, he moved over to the open cell door and stepped just inside. Jason tried to concentrate on his Bible, but all he could hear was blood pumping in his ears. The big man did not move.

"Think that's gonna pertect ya?"

"I'm sorry?"

"You think that book is gonna save you, pertect you in here?"

"It helps to have it near me."

"I say, you think it'll *pertect* you?!"

"I believe...these words can do...anything."

The big man laughed. "Hey, let's see what your book can do for you now."

Inmates were gathering outside Jason's cell. Some were silent; wide-eyed and fascinated. Others laughed. One man passed, craned his neck to look inside, and then turned away, shaking his head in disgust. Only a portion of the cell interior was visible through the crush of bodies outside, revealing a glimpse of two figures on the concrete cell floor. The big man was on his knees, his hands on Jason's Bible, which lay upon his bunk. Jason, beside him on one knee, held one hand on his Bible and the other on the man's shoulder. Jason spoke softly into his ear. The big man listened intently. And he was smiling.

CHAPTER FIVE

"**G**OMMI, IF YOU THINK ABOUT SOMETHING ELSE, THE TIME will go faster."

Jackie glanced at J.J., looking very small in this big prison waiting area. He was so calm and trusting, just waiting for his daddy to come back home. Jackie realized that his Gommi had probably been making them all nervous with her pacing, but she simply could not sit still. Jason was so close. Could it be that he really would be coming through those doors and back home to them? Jackie looked around the waiting area and remembered the first time she had been seated here, waiting to talk to Jason through those awful glass partitions. Just nine days ago? She shuddered and was grateful that the room was relatively empty and quiet this early evening. And then Jackie began to pace again.

"Come sit over here with us," Stephanie offered. "Then you can see Jason the minute he comes out."

Larry drawled, "You are about to wear a hole in that floor, Honey."

Jackie took a steadying breath, glanced at the clock again, and sat beside Stephanie, her eyes fixed on the massive metal door at the end of the hallway. Stephanie gave her arm a reassuring squeeze and turned to J.J.

"J.J., where you want to take Daddy for dinner?"

"Ummmm...Spin-a-Pin."

"You really think we ought to take him to a bowling alley on his first night home? Let's take him some place really nice to eat."

J.J. considered this for a moment, then turned solemnly to his mom. "Okay, then; Baskin-Robbins."

Jackie was taking all this in. This beautiful girl who married her son was someone to reckon with. She was sweet and gentle and beautiful. But now, in the midst of all the horror, she was revealing herself to have an iron core that would not be bent.

Stephanie laughed at the ice cream parlor suggestion and offered, "How 'bout we let Daddy decide?"

"Mommy, will Daddy eat with us from now on?"

J.J. looked to his mommy. Larry and Jackie listened. After a moment, Stephanie spoke.

"When we love somebody, they're always with us. Even when we can't see them with our eyes, we see them in our mind and heart, don't we? So let's just look at Daddy and see him as much as we can. Look hard as we can. And when he's at work or...when he's not right in front of us, he'll still be with us."

J.J. considered this, and then nodded in agreement. Jackie smiled. Suddenly the door opened with a metallic rasp and a woman dressed in a black suit appeared, speaking to an unseen figure behind her.

"You know your family's been waiting for you for some time," the woman said. "Let's see if we can get you home to them tonight."

She held the door open and a small, sad man with a moustache entered, and followed the woman across the room and out the front door. J.J. noticed that his suit did not fit him. They waited.

Again, the door pushed open, and this time, a pleasant-looking chaplain stuck his head out, looked around, smiled and then disappeared. Stephanie looked away in disappointment only to see J.J. bolt across the floor. She turned just in time to see Jason come through the door that the chaplain held open. J.J. leapt into his daddy's arms. And Jason held him and held him without saying a word, eventually sinking to the floor, but still holding his son. This seemed as if it would go on forever, but then J.J. grabbed Daddy's head in his tiny hands, pushing his face away. Jason swallowed hard and managed a smile.

"Hey, Mister, what are you doing to me?"

J.J. just held his daddy's face and stared. "I'm looking at you. Hard as I can."

Jason took his son's face gently into his own hands, and they sat on the prison floor, just looking at one another. Hard as they can.

Beams cut through the woods, laying long misty slats of light between the trees. If only the van would keep driving. But then the screaming began, voices all talking at once and in unknown languages. And then the gun exploded, spraying black fluid across the side of the white van. Sensing something behind him, Jason turned to see a stainless steel table gleaming in the midst of the woods, two lights shining mercilessly on the lifeless body laid out upon it. The man was covered with dried mud and bits of gravel and brush, and his clothes had been partially cut away from his body. His face was turned to Jason at an odd angle. As Jason approached, he could see the lips were pulled back from the teeth; the first signs of rigor mortis. The fingers, too, had begun to draw up. On the man's far shoulder, a gaping wound was edged in charred blackness. And then the man opened his eyes and looked right at Jason.

Stephanie was sitting up in bed by the time Jason emitted the second scream. She did not try to hold him, but rather touched him gently, saying over and over, "Jason, you're home. You're home now, Baby. It's all over. You're home, Jason, you are home."

Jason looked at his wife but did not appear to recognize her. He pulled away, toward his side of the bed and pushed her reaching arms back. In the half light she looked odd; different. Why did she keep reaching for him? He scooted further away and swung around, attempting to get off the bed. And there, reaching from the closet, was the corpse of Juan Carlos Reymundo.

Jason screamed, opened his eyes, and jerked to a sitting position in the bed. He could not get away, not anywhere. It was with him, it was after him, it would never go away.

Stephanie held him tight. "It's me Jason, it's me. Look at me, Jason, it's me. Look at me. Jason, I'm right here. I'm right here."

Jason looked raggedly about the bedroom, checking every corner, and clasping hard to Stephanie. If Reymundo was here, Jason would grab Steph and drag her from the room before the dead man could get them. Jason did not even realize he was still screaming until J.J. darted into the room in his blue cowpoke pajamas. J.J. and Stephanie held onto Jason until the screaming stopped, and then they held him until he stopped crying.

The concrete slab had been poured before Jason was arrested, the living room pool in its very center. Soon now the framing would be finished. One crew was working on the house itself; another working with the fieldstone to complete the massive rock fence that would surround the house and grounds, allowing Jackie's beloved dogs to run, protected, within its bounds. Today it all appeared a patchwork of building materials, equipment, and workers, but

Jason's trained eye could see the house as it would be; nestled on the hillside, solid and sprawling, and connected to the earth as if it was always meant to be here. Jackie had shown little interest in her dream house since Jason's release. But for Jason, it was more than a house; it was a mission.

Weeks before the incident, when Jason told Stephanie he intended to enter the ministry, just like his big brother Jim, she said not a word. She didn't have to. Stephanie supported Jason's dreams, and that was empowering to them both. They did discuss what this would mean in terms of family, time, and income. Together, they decided Jason would keep his construction business. It had taken him years to build it and it was not just a business to him, it was something that he loved to do. It was also a career for which he had natural instincts and a sturdy business sense. On one hand it seemed a no-brainer: Two careers! But they realized it would demand twice the work, twice the dedication, and more hours than a day held. Especially during the time in which Jason was studying for the ministry, the entire family would be stretched. They also knew that, if the past had taught them anything, Satan would become overly active whenever they were in reach of something good, especially if it was in service of others, and in celebration of the gifts loaned by God. And this was, quite literally, how they viewed it. Satan, to Jason and Jackie and their families, was truly an entity. Too often they had seen him frolic and cavort, sticking pins and breaking bones, strewing the way with endless obstacles as they followed their passions and true paths. "Satan don't want us to do good works," Jackie had said. "He becomes especially agitated as we get close to accomplishing something great." And this philosophy, rather than hindering, actually helped. Picturing

Satan as a conscious, focused, relentless force helped them face and deny him. Knowing him empowered them. The monster you do not see is so much worse than the monster that is known. And so they acknowledged him and his power. But they also acknowledged that Satan's power was limited. And they knew that he was used, in the bigger scheme of things, to test and strengthen us, and ultimately, that he must flee from the name of Jesus Christ. Though we ourselves are weak, we can access unlimited protection. So from the time they were little boys, both Jim and Jason, when faced with evil, would say, "Satan, you must leave this place. In the name of Jesus Christ, be gone." And they both knew that it might take some time and there would be trials and often fractures in their faith. But if they faced him squarely, put him soundly in his place, and never backed down, that eventually he must go. And somewhere in the grand scheme of things, the world would be a better place for it all.

Stop working on Mom's house? No way! This is a celebration of God's beauty and one woman's faith in him. This house is a testament to God's bounty and artistry. Jason did not know when or how, but it was his intention to finish his Mom's home. And he knew that *intention*, combined with prayer, was an awesome combination. *I can do all things through Christ, which strengtheneth me*. All things. Wow. That is one powerful sound bite!

The change in Jackie since Jason's release on bond had been remarkable, and Jason did not know whether to applaud it or be concerned. Unhappy with legal counsel and unable to wait patiently through these months leading up to the trial, Jackie had turned herself into something of a lawyer. She was never without her laptop, and pursued every lead she could uncover. Jackie researched murder cases and their defenses, self defense cases and their defenses, insanity cases and their defenses. Not only did she research Georgia laws and Georgia cases, but those in other states as well. She pored endlessly over law books, contacted officials, scheduled appointments and networked endlessly. The Carpenter living room became command central, and Post-It notes covered the walls and tables. Significantly, Jackie heard mention of the Georgia Stand-Your-Ground Law on an early morning news show. Digging into its background, she found that this law stated that a person, on their own property, was not required by law to retreat if someone entered without invitation. No, a man on his own property could stand his ground. And wasn't that exactly what Jason did, she'd ask over and over? He stood his ground! This, she believed, would be their defense in the courtroom. Jackie followed every lead, and searched through every volume for answers. But neither Jackie nor her family had yet realized, that all this time, she was looking in the wrong book.

One thing that fueled Jackie's campaign was the fact that the press was mangling the truth horribly. Media reports led to blogs and online comments and ramblings and posts about racial killings and spoiled rich kids and the wealthy who owned the courts. Worse, the entire family was under a gag order and unable to say a thing in Jason's defense. Nor were they allowed to set straight one single inaccuracy or outright lie. Anything they said, they were correctly warned, could be twisted and come back to hurt Jason's case. So now Jason was being tried in the courts of public opinion and found guilty.

He fretted over his mom and her single-minded dedication to his case. She had lost a significant amount of weight and hardly seem to sleep at all. She called at all hours and Stephanie noticed that many of her emails came in at 1 am, 2am, 4am, as well as all throughout the day and evening. Jackie's jaw was set but her eyes had a far-off look and her hands shook. It seemed she could only talk about and think about one thing. She was ferocious in her determination. Jason loved his mom and her strong, beautiful spirit. But he worried over what her concern for him was doing. Jason, for all the horror he was experiencing, did not want the weight shared with his beloved family. He did not know what he could do to help. But he did know this: He could build. And so he did.

Jackie was concerned about Jason. He had thrown himself into supervising the construction of her new home with a furious energy. And he had decided to continue to pursue his desire to study for, and enter, the ministry. And she admired this dedication, but the bottom line was this: He was juggling two careers, and over his head hung a Sword of Damocles that grew heavier each day. He had left the county prison almost twenty pounds lighter than when he entered. She - none of them - had any details of what had happened to him inside. He refused to talk about it. The only details he shared had to do with ministering to some of the inmates. Jason read the Bible that Ellis had brought to him in prison. He gained his strength from it and rejected even the idea of keeping it closed. Perhaps it was only curiosity at first, but something about this young man who refused to grow hard, as well as refusing to be broken, had intrigued some of the inmates, even the "worst of the worst" in Cell Block A. During his first meal after being released on bond, Jason brought smiles to the family as he shoveled away portion after portion of fattening food at his favorite restaurant. But he had not returned to his normal weight. And he always seemed to be working. Jackie loved her children so very much. She often found herself dwelling on the fact that, the worst pain a mortal can experience, is seeing someone they love suffer, and being unable to do anything about it. Well, if it was humanly possible, she *would* do something about it! She worked day and night, researching every aspect of Jason's case and similar ones. Ellis had informed the family of his own limitations and was actively searching for the best criminal trial lawyer that could be found. Jackie wanted to be prepared when this man was revealed to them. And so, she let not one second pass that was not in active pursuit of answers, clues, and the one missing piece of the puzzle that would make this nightmare go away. Jason had become the center of a media frenzy; just the type of case that made headlines: Rich against poor or Caucasian against ethnic seemed to be the theme of every article, blog, and post, and the press practically drooled and grinned each time they found a gory new angle. Jackie finally learned what "If It Bleeds, It Leads" meant in the press. But above all, she was concerned about Jason and the ultimate horror of him being taken away from his family. For all she knew, he could go to jail forever, or even be put to death. The adrenalin pumped through her system and set her on fire. She had to act; had to do something. But what? There was only one thing that she knew to do, and that was to research, contact, learn, push, push, and push. She could work. And so she did.

CHAPTER SIX

CYNTHIA WATCHED JACKIE AS THEY STROLLED THROUGH THE aisles. Jackie's hair was pinned back casually, not at all like the careful hairstyles of old, and the light layer of makeup did little to hide the dark, sunken areas around her eyes. Cynthia flipped aside her festive red cape and joined arms with her friend. Jackie didn't seem to notice. Cynthia was a striking and formidable woman. Her ebony skin, strong features, and mass of braids complimented a positively glorious smile. But in this rare moment, she was not smiling. They walked on. Cynthia eyed Jackie closely.

"I can't get used to it," Cynthia purred in her heavy accent.

Nothing. They walked a bit further.

Cynthia nudged Jackie with her elbow. "Bet you are wondering what it is I cannot get used to."

"The cold weather?" Jackie wondered where the summer had gone.

"No. Well, yes; that too. But what I cannot get used to, since you are so interested, is how you sell Jesus in the stores here. Christmas come and Baby Jesus is in all the windows. Then come December 26 - boom - he's 75% off for After Christmas Sale."

Jackie registered a tiny smile and looked around. Here they were in the crush of after Christmas shopping; discounts and packages and crowds all around her and she had hardly noticed. The holiday music infusing the shop seemed out of place and the bright lights and colors bothered her eyes. Jackie stopped and turned to her friend.

"Cynthia, I just can't enjoy this -- not today."

"That's 'cause you're not seeing what's all around you," Cynthia remarked while pointing out a glittery countertop display. "Look at this pretty scene with Santa and his red suit and the snow. In Jamaica we don't have that."

"You don't have Santa Claus?"

"Well, yes, we have Santa, but no snow. We see a fat man in a red suit with white flakes on his shoulder, we just think dandruff."

And with this, Jackie finally laughed and Cynthia threw back her head and joined in.

Jackie took Cynthia's hand in hers. "Aw, Sweetie, I appreciate what you're trying to do, but I can't keep my mind off the arraignment. After waiting all these months, he's there -- right now -- standing in front of that judge and --"

"Okay, so let's talk about it then. You want to go be with him?"

"I can't; only Jason and his attorneys are allowed."

"So you want to do what you cannot do. *Stop that!* And what would you do if you *could* be there?"

"Nothing," Jackie admitted.

"That's right. So why don't you just do nothing here with me and let the law people do their job." They began to stroll down the crowded aisles again. "Tell me about this new lawyer man."

"Mitchell Kane. Ellis says he's the best. He has a really good track record in mur- in cases like Jason's. He grew up around here. He's a magician--"

"Musician?"

"Magician."

"He pull bunnies out of hats?" Cynthia inquired.

"I guess so."

"And cut people in half with a saw?"

"Maybe."

"And make folks disappear?"

"Yeah."

"I think I have a job for Mr. Kane after this trial is done." And, laughing, Cynthia bolted around a counter, peering impishly at Jackie over a family of plush snowmen.

Jackie toyed distractedly with a tiny snow covered village, one with twinkling lights inside. "I just don't like having Jason around that courthouse for any reason. I'll be better when he's back home."

"You think it gonna make Jason happy to see his mommy's face all wrinkly with worry? C'mon; we're here with all the pretty stuff. Might as well do something to make us smile."

Gazing at Cynthia's familiar insistent expression, Jackie finally relented and spoke. "Tell you what: Let me stop by the ladies' room, and then we'll get something to eat. Something fattening. My treat."

"Good idea. I'll wait here and see if I can find something for 100% off!"

And with that, Cynthia began to check out price tags in a greedily exaggerated manner. Jackie, feeling a bit lighter, grinned and turned on her heels, heading for the back of the store.

Cynthia watched her dear friend disappear into the crowd, then turned her attention to a little chalet, with pristine snow on the roof and a tiny family gazing out from the parlor window. She liked the way their house appeared so complete and cozy; she could see a rug and furniture and a glow in the fireplace. This would be some-thing happy for Jackie to look at, and remember their shopping trip together. Cynthia made her way to a checkout lane and stood behind a woman with a stroller. Gazing at the mother and child, she recalled how many tough times Jackie had faced in her life. But never, never had she seen her so dangerously worn. It seemed as if Satan had taken a particular interest in the Carpenter/Veitch family. That would make some kind of hateful sense, she mused. These are good people, happy and successful people; an ethical family with a strong faith in God. What better people to tear down? The line began to move forward. No, he will not win. He will push and tear, but he will not win. And she would do battle in prayer and if necessary, wrestle the old demon to the ground with her very hands before she would see him win. This was the Old One; the darkness from the pit. He was strong, but he would not win.

An odd sound caused Cynthia to glance over her shoulder. And just as she did, a shopper dropped her bags unceremoniously to the floor and bolted across a back aisle. Another woman followed quickly. How bizarre. Maybe there's a sale.

Slowly Cynthia moved out of the queue. She placed the little chalet on the nearest countertop and began to walk to the back of the store. Then she began to run.

Jackie was slumped before a colorful glass display case, her knees pulled to her chin, and her cell phone gripped in one hand. The contents of her purse were strewn about. Cynthia moved aside the customers who had surrounded her, and joined Jackie on the floor. She pulled near, and together they sat for a moment in this little corner, tinkly music and blinking lights around them. Cynthia made a gentle attempt to retrieve Jackie's phone, but she held it tight. Still, she managed to hit the desired buttons and the name M. Kane lit the screen. Jackie just stared off.

"Jackie, my precious, I need for you to talk to me if you can. Tell me what it is. Just talk to me."

After a moment, Jackie turned to Cynthia, then looked at her phone, then back to Cynthia. Slowly she began to speak. "District Attorney Pitt told the Grand Jury today that she wants to indict Jason for felony murder."

"Yes, we all know that." Cynthia kept her voice soft, gentle. Soon Jackie began to speak again, but the words were punctuated with chokes and swallows, as tears welled and fell.

"...and felony possession and aggravated assault and....*five charges now*. And the judge asked her again to please, please reduce the charge and she insisted - *insisted* - that they try Jason on the worst possible charges. Cynthia, who is this woman?! Who is Evelyn Pitt? Why is she trying to...." And the sobs took over and silenced her.

Cynthia took both of Jackie's hands and held them in her own. "Aaaaah, me! So God has given you another load to bear. But He knows what you can stand, and will not give you a mountain that is too high. And He has given you people who love you, and we *will not leave you*. So. We *do*. That's it; we just *do*. Let's get started on this climb. What's next?"

"Kane wants to see us in his office."

Kane was late. Jackie sat in a comfortable chair in his quietly carpeted office, her ever-present Bible in her lap, with Larry seated to her right, then Stephanie, then Jason. Ellis sat in a chair behind them, near the door. They stared at Kane's empty desk. Beyond it, the afternoon sun was reaching through half-closed blinds. Larry lifted his arm and checked his watch. The sound of his movement, fabric rustling against fabric, was unnaturally loud. They waited.

"Good morning, good morning, good morning!" Kane burst in from behind them and strode to his desk, breathing heavily. This was not what they were expecting. A tall, dark-skinned man in a sweaty jogging suit lifted a bottle of water to his mouth and drank loudly. They could hardly make out his face; a hood was pulled over his head. Kane guzzled his water, then pushed back the hood with his free hand. His face was wet and he wore a skull cap. Then he dove into his chair, arms and legs splayed expansively, and peeled the cap off to reveal close-cropped hair. Breathing loudly and checking his pulse, he still had not spoken further. This was the man who would save Jason? This was their hope? He seemed more interested in his workout and heart rate than his clients; his office bookshelves were filled with toys and magic tricks. What were they thinking?

Jackie bolted upright. "Mr. Kane? Mr. Kane, before we even begin, can you tell me one positive thing about this case?

Kane wiped his face on his cap and took one more gulp of water, carefully screwing the cap back on. He spoke in measured tones. "Jackie, what you want me to say to you is this will all be over soon; that Jason will be exonerated from all charges, and he will be totally free to go back home to his family. I can't tell you that."

Jason spoke up. "Then, Mr. Kane, what can you tell us?"

"I can tell you that District Attorney Pitt has offered to drop the felony murder charge for a voluntary manslaughter charge."

It was as if the family had been given a shot of adrenalin. The entire mood of the room seemed to brighten. So Ellis was right! This was the miracle man he'd told them about. Kane continued.

"The judge has agreed to a bench trial, which means the media will not be allowed in the courtroom; the judge will decide the case."

"Why, why this change?" Jackie asked.

"It all goes back to Deputy Clayton Book. He's the primary reason Jason was charged with felony murder in the first place. But Deputy Book has been terminated."

Jackie and Jason spoke at the same time. "Fired?" "Why?"

Leaning forward, Kane's voice was becoming energized. "Soon as the sheriff found out Deputy Book had carried Mr. Morales and Mr. Lerma back to the alleged crime scene and spoken to the news about the incident, he started to sweat. It looked like he was attempting to cover something up --"

"Which he was!" Jackie interrupted.

"--so the sheriff terminated Deputy Book before he could give the department a black eye. And since the DA's case was built on Book's accusations, this could weaken their case considerably in a jury trial."

Stephanie could not contain herself. "So, so," she stammered, "so they don't have a case? They're dropping the charges?"

"Not by a long shot." Kane's tone abruptly changed. "This information about Deputy Book probably influenced Pitt's decision to offer this plea bargain -- which means you get to accept a lesser charge -- and to a bench trial, which means the public and the media will not be in attendance."

"What...I don't..." Stephanie began.

Jason turned to his wife. "I think what he is trying to tell us is..."

Jackie broke in. "Just say it. Just talk to us like people!"

Kane took a deep breath and eyed those in the room steadily. "District Attorney Pitt and Judge Overby have agreed to reduce the felony murder charge to voluntary manslaughter and you will serve three to five years, or if you do not accept his plea bargain, the judge will try you in a bench trial and find you guilty of nothing less than voluntary manslaughter. Either way, you *are* going to prison and most probably for three years. And he wants your decision soon."

Jason lurched toward the window and stood with his back to the room. Jackie, her face hard, rose slowly and addressed Kane. "Let me make sure I understand this. The only reason all this is happening to Jason is because this Deputy Clayton Book lied, and now everyone, including the sheriff and the DA and the judge *know* that he lied, but they still won't let Jason go?"

Kane could see the months of rage and pain rising to the surface and attempted to calm Jackie with his voice. He spoke softly to the room, but kept his eyes on the trembling woman standing before him.

"Jackie, if he takes the plea bargain, he won't get more than three years. If he takes the jury trial, there's a 50/50 chance he'll go to prison for at least thirty."

Larry looked up to see his wife's head droop; she seemed to be drawn downward. Then, abruptly, her head snapped up and she eyed Kane as she slowly began to walk around his desk and toward him.

"Can you tell me why Jason's case just becomes weaker every time it strengthens itself? Can you tell me why the termination of this deputy hurt the DA but didn't help us at all? Can you tell me why my son should go to jail? Let me tell you why my son should *not* go to jail--" Jackie could hear Ellis saying something to her, but she just raised her volume and continued. "He has a seven year old son who needs him. He has a wife who depends on him. He is no threat to society. He has no prior record. He is innocent. He is innocent. *He is innocent!"*

As Jackie continued to rail and Ellis tried to calm her, Larry found himself standing. Enough. This was enough. Time he took care of his family. With each sentence, Larry's voice was raised to be heard over Jackie's.

"Well, I just think Jason needs to listen to these attorneys and take their advice!" Larry shouted. "They know what's best for him." Jackie, matching his volume, turned to glare at Larry, but he continued to shout right along with her. "You need to go ahead and get this over with; serve the time and you'll be back home before you know it. Three years is not much compared to thirty. I just think--"

Jackie wheeled on Larry, as both Ellis and Kane tried to calm them. "You think? *You think?!* You want him to go to jail for something he didn't do?"

"I want him to pay up and get it over with!"

"Pay up? Pay up?!"

"I think he needs to--"

"You're not his father!"

Stillness. Except for the sound of Stephanie softly crying, all was still. Larry's face registered the pain of someone who had been physically wounded. Jackie, unable to process her feelings of violence and rage, just stood shaking. Kane averted his eyes and Ellis held his hand tight to his mouth. Just then, Jason turned from the window. Tears ran down his hollow cheeks. He walked directly to Jackie and took her arms in his two hands. She looked at him with something akin to fear. Then he drew his mom near and held her. She almost collapsed, but he held her firmly until she returned his hug with her left hand; her right still clutching her Bible. When she had calmed a bit, he held her by the shoulders and gave her a smile. Then he moved around Stephanie and past Ellis, who was still standing. Larry was facing away, with his hands shoved in his pockets. Jason stared at his back for just one moment, then slid a hand around his neck. He leaned his head on Larry's shoulder and spoke quietly into his ear.

"You know I love you."

Larry made no sound, but through his clenched jaw he managed to mouth the words, "Me, too."

Then Jason stood beside his wife, taking her hand.

"When we finish with the trial, whether it be a bench trial or a jury trial, Mr. Kane, you'll go home to your wife and family. Ellis, you will go home to your wife, and Larry, you will go home to Mom. I have to make this decision. Me and Steph. Let's go home."

They entered the vehicle without saying a word; without looking at each other. Both were still stunned. Somewhere, under the flat, dead feeling, Jackie sensed something had been broken that could never be repaired. She couldn't begin to justify why she had lashed out at Larry as she did. It just didn't seem to matter now. Nothing did.

Larry did not start the engine. Instead, he got out, and walked to the other side, opening Jackie's door. As he bent forward into the passenger side, she flinched. He grabbed her face and held it still, pressing his lips to her forehead, and holding them there until he felt her relax. Then he stood, shut her door, walked around, got in, and started the engine.

"My rock," she thought. "My rock."

Rolling over in bed, the flat of his hand hit her pillow. This pulled Larry from sleep. Jackie was not in bed. Straining his eyes, he saw the French doors opened and Jackie framed against a brilliant night sky. An icy breeze was gently swirling the curtains, but Jackie didn't seem to notice. She leaned against the door frame, her face turned out of the room and toward the night. Larry cleared his throat, then spoke quietly.

"Honey?"

Jackie spoke but did not turn to him. "I don't even know her name."

"What?"

"A boy died out on that construction site. And he has a mother. They won't even tell me her name. Did she get a phone call like us; middle of the night? I was wondering if she's sitting up right now. I don't even know her name."

"We have a big decision to make," Jason explained. He and Stephanie were seated on J.J.'s bed. It was time to tuck him in. And it was time to explain some things to him. "See, J.J.," Jason continued steadily, "because a man died, even though it was an accident, there are people who want to be absolutely sure that I didn't mean to harm him."

"And they have given us a choice," Stephanie picked up the thread. "If we decide to take their offer, and say that it was Daddy's fault, but it was an accident, then he will go to jail. For three years."

J.J. was clearly alarmed. "Three years! Don't do it!"

"But J.J, if he takes the other choice, and this choice is called a *trial*--"

Jason chimed in, "--then one of two things will happen. They might let me come right back home and stay home always. Or they might make me go to jail...for...for a long time."

"For a long, long time, Daddy?"

Jason answered truthfully, "For thirty years."

J.J. pondered this for a moment, then spoke solemnly. "It's a big decision."

"But it's not your decision," Stephanie changed her tone and stood briskly, "so we don't want you worrying about it. We just want you to know what's happening."

"Now," said Jason, rubbing his hands together, "Bedtime for all the munchkins in this house!"

Steph helped J.J. to snuggle under the covers, as Jason retrieved a large Bible filled with richly colored pictures, and settled down for story time. J.J. truly enjoyed hearing about the Bible, and possessed an innate instinct which allowed him to bridge time, and see the stories in a very contemporary manner.

"When last we left our heroes," Jason began, "we were in the Book of Psalms. Remember what *psalms* means?

"Songs!"

"Right, J.J., songs, and--"

"Daddy."

"Yes."

"Tonight, read me about the flood."

"You want to hear about Noah and the flood?"

"Yessir."

"You're sure? Right before bedtime? It's all about rain and terrible flood and days of scary darkness."

"I'm sure."

"Why, Honey?"

"Because after the flood, there was a rainbow."

Bojangles galloped along the edge of the lake, challenging the geese who floated, unconcerned, just a few feet away. Stephanie brought bread crumbs for the geese and treats for Bojangles. She took J.J.'s gloved hand and placed some crumbs in it, then watched as he threw them. They fell short and Bojangles gobbled them off the shoreline.

"Mom, Steph and I have come to a decision about the plea bargain." Jason sat on a park bench, watching his wife and child walk along the lake; his mom stood, hands in coat pockets, looking out at the chilly grey water. " Neither of us can get any peace about a bench trial. I know that I'm risking going to jail for thirty years by taking a jury trial. But Mom, we haven't been able to say a word about what really happened; none of us. This story wants to be heard. Putting it all out in the open is the right thing to do. This is what gives us peace. Mom, we're going to trial."

Jackie turned and silently walked away from the shore. Not even Bojangles saw her leave.

CHAPTER SEVEN

MONTHS OF RELENTLESS RESEARCH HAD LEFT JACKIE'S LIVING room a war zone. Every possible space, including the folding table she'd had Larry set up mid-room, was weighed down with volumes, records, transcripts, notes, and reference books. She had a network of phones and computers. No one was allowed to touch anything. On this night in late winter, Debbie was seated in a dining room chair to Jackie's right, and was peering through her glasses at a heavy, leather-bound volume. Jackie was glued to her laptop; there was a relentless, machine-gun flow to her speech.

"...every time I get on a government site this thing slows down and I know that's not just coincidence; every time I start closing in on something solid, they slow it down or it crashes on me--"

Debbie began to quote from the volume before her. "The Georgia Stand-Your-Ground Law says that you have the right to guard your property bearing arms and--"

Jackie lifted a thin hand and pushed her glasses back up on her nose. Her wedding rings had fallen off so often that she no longer wore them. "I know that, Debbie; we need to find out if Deputy Book filed his report before he spoke with Morales and Lerma. Quit trying to get me off track!"

"I just thought you wanted to know if Pitt and Crutcher--"

"*Not Crutcher and not Pitt*; we're trying to find out if *Book*--" Debbie's cell began to ring. "Send it to voicemail! --trying to find out if Book--"

As the doorbell began to ring, Debbie rose, but heard Larry shout, "I'll get it!" and seated herself again. Finally her cell stopped ringing. Hearing voices in the entry hall, Debbie turned just in time to see Larry usher Ellis into the room.

Jackie turned, snapped off a quick, "Can you two talk in some other part of the house?" and returned to her laptop.

"Sweetie." Larry began. "Sweetheart? Ellis has something he needs to tell you."

"Well, Ellis, if it's bad news, you'll just have to wait your turn."

"It's about the trial and--"

Jackie sat working, her back to him. "Talk, Ellis; just say it."

Ellis remained framed in the doorway with his heavy coat still on. He began hesitantly. "Kane has asked that you - all of us - certain things.... Uh, Kane feels - we all feel -- that you shouldn't bring your Bible into the courtroom." Jackie typed and typed. "If there are non-believers among the jury members, and they see you with your Bible, it might offend them." Typing. "They could hold it against you. They could hold it against Jason." Jackie never missed a key. "Well, that was the main thing that I...I'll just go over the rest with Larry and--"

Before Ellis could make his escape, Jackie had spun in her chair and nailed him with a steady gaze. She spoke casually at first. " What else do you want, Ellis? Want me to change my hair? This length might offend somebody. And what color outfit do I wear? Blue might offend someone, but red's sure to set somebody off!

And what if we do forget the Bible for these non-believers? What about the believers? I guess it just comes down to who I want to offend, because either way, I will offend someone! Thank you, Ellis, I just didn't have enough going on in my life right now."

And with that, she turned back to her work. Larry gently led Ellis out of the room. Watching her cousin just then, Debbie had felt a huge weight grow in her heart and a lump swell in her throat. Jackie was so thin and frail, yet seemed possessed by a manic drive that would not set her free. It was as if some huge beast had her within its jaws and constantly shook her, never letting her rest. Sherry leaned forward and spoke. "Honey, why don't you take a rest and--"

"Get out."

"Wha-what?"

"Get out get out get out of my house *now*!"

Larry and Ellis rushed back into the room to find Jackie sitting alone and typing.

Someone was crying. Jackie could hear them, very nearby, but did not recognize the voice. She tried to lift her eyelids as well as the heavy covers. Pulling herself to the edge of the bed, she crawled onto the floor and tried to stand, but fell to her side. The crying was closer and she felt breath on her face. Who was crying? It was so very dark or maybe she had not opened her eyes. She would crawl to the prayer closet and be safe there.

Jackie had turned a walk-in closet into a prayer closet. Soon after she had confronted God in Jim's church, she had made a prayer closet at home. Having told God that she was rejecting Him as her source of peace, had inexplicably made her feel closer to Him. If she had been able to think clearly, perhaps she would have realized that made little sense, just as taking the reins of Jason's trial into her own hands, but forever clutching her Bible made little sense. One might wonder if using the prayer closet as her refuge, even as she rejected God in many ways, might be the little grain of mustard seed that represented her still-living faith. Perhaps holding onto the Bible, even in the darkest moments of doubt, kept alive that one grain, that seed of faith that Our Father tells us is all that we need. It doesn't matter how small, as long as faith is present. But all was darkness now for Jackie. And this had become the norm for her. By day man assaulted her with dead-ends, desperation, helplessness, anxiety, and hopelessness. By night, the fear fell upon her like a mindless entity; gnawing and killing and destroying and never giving her poor mind a moment's refuge. Still, miraculously, the lessons of her childhood dwelt within her heart: *Thou shalt not be afraid for the terror by night; nor for the arrow that flieth by day.* And so she crawled to her prayer closet.

The crying was in the hallway now. Jackie's hair was wet and plastered to her face. Her hands and feet were numb. Her hand slid wetly on the tile floor, and she wondered if she had cut her hand and was leaving a trail of blood. Why couldn't she see? The crying was ahead of her again. She followed. A yellow glow appeared. It was the little night light that she used to make her way to the prayer closet in the dark. This had occurred so often before, yet the terror of it was always new. If she could only make it to the closet, she would pray for strength. Finally, she could see her goal. And the whimpering and crying were ahead. These heartbreaking cries were coming from her prayer closet, leading her on through the darkness. One more, one more, one hand before the other...plant the knees and drag the legs. And she was there.

Bojangles sat inside Jackie's prayer closet, whining softly. Though this had never happened before, she accepted his guidance without question. "Animals are angels," Jackie thought. "Angels." She and her little angel sat within the tiny room and asked for help. All she had the energy to say was, "Here I am, Lord. Plug me in to life support." And He gently took her by the hand and turned her eyes to Him until peace came. Though she had turned her eyes to man and what man could do for her, though she had turned away from God, He had never left her. Though she felt herself lost and hopeless, she was being surely led; burned away and reduced to cinders, so that she could be reborn.

"I've passed that courthouse twice now," Jackie murmured. How could she have become so lost? She'd been to Kane's office many times before, sometimes with Larry but often alone. Mitchell Kane and his assistant Emily continuously told her that she was not needed, but she saw nothing moving on Jason's case, so she doggedly pursued them. "If we don't stay on them, they don't do a thing," she told Larry, "and if you won't stay on them, I will!"

Pulling back on the main road, Jackie felt a pang of guilt. Larry was her rock and her support and the most generous and kind man she had ever known. He had been a real father for her boys for most of their lives and he adored her without reservation. Once, before Jason and Stephanie had decided to take the jury trial, she had shouted at Kane and Emily that there must be something, *something* else that could be done to help them. Reluctantly, Kane admitted that a complete, mock trial could be staged - at great expense, he added - that would give them a clearer picture of what the verdict might be, should they choose a jury trial. When pressed for the amount, Kane told them it would cost at least one hundred thousand dollars. Without missing a beat, Larry told him to proceed, and brought the money to him the next day. The mock trial, lengthy and grueling, ended with Jason being convicted. And when Jason told Kane they had decided to take the jury trial after all, Kane stated flatly, "You are making the biggest mistake of your life." Today she wanted to see what Kane had done since her calls of the previous day. Jackie knew he was avoiding her, she was sure of it. She could tell by the tone in Emily's voice each time she answered Kane's office phone.

And there it was again, that same courthouse! But this couldn't be. She was in Turin now and the last time she saw it was in Senoia. Jackie made a sharp left and started around the block. This was the third time she had seen the same courthouse in three different towns! She was going to get to the bottom of this. Rounding the block, she focused on the courthouse and slowed the car down. Yes, it was the same one. How were they doing this? And then her heart skipped and doubled. There, walking up the long sidewalk to the double front doors, were Jason and Steph and J.J.! What was happening? Why wasn't anyone letting her know what was going on?! Jackie slammed on the brakes and stopped the car without pulling over, then she leapt out onto the pavement and lurched toward her family. They wouldn't keep her in the dark any longer. They'd tell her what was happening; she'd make them! She managed to reach them just before they started to climb the steps. Out of breath, she couldn't speak, but grabbed onto Jason's shoulder, spinning him around. Before her stood an attractive young stranger with a surprised look on his face. Jackie realized she was still grasping his shoulder. She looked down to see the man's little girl looking up at her with a frightened stare. The girl's mother protectively pulled her close.

A few minutes later, Jackie wondered if this incident had happened at all. She doubted it until she saw the same courthouse, this time in Sharpsburg. No. This is really happening. She gunned the engine and hit the main road, dialing the phone at the same time. Waiting for Larry to pick up, she tried to indentify the area around her, but it looked completely unfamiliar. How would she tell him to come get her if she didn't know where she was?!

Her voice was astonishingly calm and matter-of-fact when Larry answered. "Honey, I -- this is silly, but -- I turned off the wrong exit and -- Larry, Larry, I'm losing you. I don't know where I am; I was trying to find Kane's office and, I'm just lost. Larry. Larry? I'm lost."

A snowfall of glass showered upon Jackie as the landscape outside her car rolled and tumbled. Larry was still on the line when they cut her out of the seatbelt and lifted her, gently, from where she hung upside down.

Jackie was napping, but she could hear everything. She could hear Stephanie playing games with J.J. and her mama telling her daddy it was time for him to go home and get some rest. Larry was talking to Cynthia about something called tea or tea cells but she did not understand it at all. And Debbie was there, too. And Jim and his sweet wife Jennifer and their little girls, Patience, Anna Grace, and Hannah. The only thought that made sense to Jackie was that she was dead and this was her funeral. It angered her that she could hear it, but could not see what was happening.

At some point, Jackie began to hear the voices of strangers and pick out conversations that she could not follow. And she felt...

things. It was as if she were being held down or tied down with tape and straps. Finally, she opened her eyes. She was in a hospital. She apparently had been there for some time. And she was tied to tubes, and needles had been stuck into her and taped securely. She began to pull the needles, slowly for she was terribly weak, out of her arms. Each freed needle would drip liquid as her arm dripped blood. The sheets were becoming quite messy, but it was time for her to leave. Abruptly, Jackie decided that she was tired and needed to sleep.

Some time later, Jackie sat up in bed, listening to her daddy. He explained that the car accident itself had done little to harm her. But when she was admitted to the hospital, they found she was in a dangerous state. Her Hemoglobin level was down to 8, and she required, among other things, a full blown transfusion. And this would be only the beginning of a long road back to physical health. But she wondered if perhaps it was all useless. Why get well? Where was her life? Why had this nightmare come and taken her family, her son, her faith? And where was God? Why had He let this happen to them? And why would He not help?

On her last day in the hospital, Jackie sat up, waiting for Larry to come and take her home. She was told that she was doing much better, but things felt just the same. Jackie lay back on the hospital pillow and stared out the window. Suddenly she heard a familiar voice behind her. Jim leaned in the door, smiling.

"My pretty mom 'bout ready to go back home?"

"Jim. It's good to see your face."

"And it's good to see you, looking so much better. I hear they're kicking you out of here real soon."

"Today. At eleven. That means I'll be able to eat lunch outside, a free woman." Jackie's heart darkened at that last phrase.

"Well, I won't keep you then," Jim responded in his soft voice. He pulled a chair up near his mom. "Last night, out of the clear blue, I saw words in front of my eyes. And these words were for you. The message was that you are to move into, and live in, the book of Psalms. Does that mean anything to you?"

Jackie managed a weak, bewildered smile, and shook her head.

"Me, neither. But I bet it will. So. I 'spect Larry will be here soon to pick you up. But you just remember that message; will you do that for me?"

"Move into the book of Psalms," Jackie recited obediently.

"And live there."

"And live there."

Though weak, Jackie insisted upon accompanying Larry into the drugstore when he stopped to pick up her meds. She wanted to move around freely - as freely as her weakened state would allow - and see something other than the antiseptic walls of a hospital. Larry stood at the counter beneath the neon sign that proclaimed this was a PHARMACY as she carefully strolled the aisles. At the end of one aisle was a tiny gift section, with figurines and cards. She stopped and gazed. And there, right at eye level, displayed on a small rack, was a book. Its title: *Psalm 91: God's Shield of Protection* by Peggy Joyce Ruth. Larry lifted a small white bag toward her and gestured to the door. Jackie took the book from the rack.

"And this," Jackie said. "Buy me this."

When Jim had said goodbye to the last of his congregation, he turned and walked back through the white wooden door, and down the aisle. There was still a lone figure seated inside. Quietly, he took a seat in the pew just behind her.

"Mom. Service is over."

"Can we just stay here?

"You and me?"

"All of us."

"You can if you want to."

"You spoke on Psalms today."

"Yes, Mom."

"I don't know what I'm supposed to do."

"You mean, about bringing your Bible into the courtroom?"

"Did I try too hard?"

"Do your best and let God do the rest."

"Have I?"

"Done your best?"

"Have I?"

"More."

"I feel so small."

"Maybe that's a good thing."

"Lost."

"God wants us to come to Him as little children."

"That's just what Debbie said."

"When?"

"I yelled at her."

"When?"

"A hundred years ago."

"Can I help my mom?"

"Go home. Hug your babies."

Jim reached across the pew, laying his hand gently upon her shoulder, then rose and walked quietly up the aisle, closing the door soundlessly behind him. After a moment, Jackie leaned forward to the pew before her and rested her hand on it, then her head upon her arm. She gazed upon the crucifix above the choir loft and remembered how she had challenged her Father here, telling him that she would take care of things if He would not. Today, there was no fight. Jackie only felt surrender. She spoke.

"My Heavenly Father, I'm so tired. I've done all I know for my Jason. We all have. As much as I love him, You love him more. He is so heavy and my arms just won't hold him anymore. Take him from me. Take him into Your arms. I have nothing more to give. I give him to You. I am done."

And so Jackie Carpenter died. Stripped of her will, burned clean of all that weighed her down, she left behind her broken and worn self and arose. She had finally surrendered and become the empty vessel to be refilled. There was no doubt what was happening to her, though she had never experienced it before. The sweet release and lightness suffused her very being and she became a prism for transcendent colors and sounds. A wind seemed to rush through her and stir the pines outside the stained glass windows, casting shadows that bowed and rose. She lifted her eyes to the words above one of the windows; words she had never noticed before: *He Being Dead Yet Speaketh*. There was an innate understanding within her that everything in the past was for a reason, as would be all things in the future, whatever it held. Whatever was ahead, she would not be alone. Nor had she ever been. She was reborn.

Seated in the living room, reading the newspaper, Larry watched Jackie cross through the room, two books in her hands. Behind her trotted Bojangles. Jackie crossed through the room in the other direction. No books. Bo followed. Larry raised the paper back up and resumed his read. Again, Jackie crossed silently through the room, books in her arms, Bojangles close behind. Again, she crossed back, without books, Bo following purposefully. And back again, without the books. This time, Bojangles gave Larry a "What does it all *mean?*" look before making his exit. On her next pass, Larry spoke.

"Honey?"

"Baby."

"Did you take your meds?"

"You take yours?"

And she was gone again. Putting down the paper and rising with a groan, Larry padded across the floor and stuck his head into the den.

"Honey?"

"Cutting out Psalms."

"Those are Bibles?"

"Mmmmm-hmmmm."

"Uh...."

"Because I want Psalms with me. Until this is over. I want to be touching them. And I want verses for everyone to hold; you and Jason and Cynthia and...I want all of you to be able to hold a Psalm, so I'm cutting them out."

"You could just copy 'em."

"Nope. No copies. We'll buy more Bibles. God won't mind."

And leaving her snipping away, Larry went back to his couch and newspaper. After a moment, Jackie called to him.

"Baby? Bring me your Bible."

He just kept on reading.

CHAPTER EIGHT

TRIAL - DAY ONE

JACKIE CARPENTER, HER BIBLE HELD HIGH AND WEARING A vibrant red suit, pumped up the yawning staircase to the heavy copper courthouse doors. She never slowed her gait, as Larry yanked the doors open, allowing her to slip through. Inside, two more staircases echoed with the determined sound of her black pumps. Larry swept open the door to the courtroom itself, and Jackie stepped inside.

It took her breath away. This was unlike anything she had ever seen, save for the occasional Hollywood blockbuster. Ornate woodwork, imposing chandeliers, and soaring marble walls cradled hundreds of people who were plastered into every crevice. Far beyond the seated crowd, she could make out the county seal, the elevated judge's seat, and the cluster of officials, deputies, and guards milling about. Just inside the chamber, and to her left and right, cameramen and reporters became galvanized upon her entrance. Like a wave, beginning in the back and moving up the benches to the front of the room, spectators turned backward, to gaze upon her. Some recognized Jackie, some were only curious, but this cavernous room, the surge of humanity, and the sudden attention, took all the wind from her lungs. Her intention was shaken and she was stilled.

Then, just as suddenly, she rose up again. Larry saw the slight adjustment to her shoulders and chin, and almost smiled. "Hey, nobody said this was gonna be easy," she thought. "But we will get through it."

And so she turned and walked toward the aisle leading to the front, where she had been told she would be sitting with her family. Just as she entered the aisle, with Larry beside her, a young woman leaned out and caught her attention. The girl, seated in the back bench and to their left, was holding a piece of paper between the fingers of both hands and lifted it up for Jackie to see. Uneasy about what this strange young person had to share with her, she nevertheless slowed her gait and allowed her eyes to focus.

It was a page from a Bible. Psalm 91 to be exact. "But how--" Jackie's mind tumbled. "Who is she--and how did she--?" The warmth of emotion and gratitude filled her chest and eyes, and catching her breath again, she smiled at this radiant young woman. As Jackie turned, a man to her right lifted his arms toward her. In his hands, a page from a Bible; from Psalms. Slowly, Jackie made her way up the aisle, Larry close by her side. As she reached each row, smiling people turned to her and lifted their Bible pages. Some had specific passages lined in red or blue, some did not. Some were held by folks she had never seen, others by family and friends. On and on they walked through a sea of gently undulating white. There was Debbie and two friends, all holding their pages for her to see. And here was Cynthia, and both she and her husband smiled as they lifted their Psalms high. There was an old high school classmate and here two more sweet people she did not know. On Jackie and Larry traveled, occasionally stopping to touch an arm or share a smile or manage a quiet thanks. On they walked, through God's promise of protection, lifted heavenward like ivory flags waving on this spring morning.

And then they were seated. Beside them were Stephanie and Jim. Before them, at a sturdy wooden table, were Ellis, Jason, and Mitchell Kane. All three men wore suits. Jason turned and smiled at his family. Seated at a matching table to their right, were the two people the Carpenters and Veitches had come to know as Gus Crutcher and Prosecuting Attorney, District Attorney Evelyn Pitt. Pitt looked so delicate in her pastel suit and pink lipstick, Jackie could easily imagine Evelyn on her wedding day or driving a van full of kids to soccer practice. But not fighting to take Jackie's child away. She watched as Pitt chatted casually with Crutcher, a tiny smile playing across her lips as she spoke. Behind Pitt and Crutcher, seated in the first rows, were the men Jackie and Larry had come to recognize as Ernesto Morales and Jose Lerma. These were the men in the newscast, the men who had accused their son of killing their friend "in cold blood" as the reporter put it. They were surrounded by family who gazed and glared at Jason and Jackie and their attorneys.

A door beside the judge's bench exploded outward and a formidable man in uniform announced in a booming voice, "All rise! The Honorable Judge S. Carroll, Superior Court of the State of Georgia, Crockett County."

And through the door, which the deputy held open, emerged the judge who would soon announce Jason's fate and future. Judge Carroll was a diminutive black woman with an inscrutable expression. She marched directly to her chair, began to sit, but stopped and looked up as if she had suddenly become aware of the hundreds of people before her. "You may be seated," she declared casually. "If the jury is ready, they may join us."

The jury filed in. "They will decide our future," Jackie mused. "They sent their kids off to school this morning and gave their bosses excuses and complained about not being able to get out of jury duty. And they will sit and listen and talk among themselves and tell us what will become of the rest of our lives."

The man seated in the witness box was dressed all in black. His skin-hugging shirt seemed almost unable to hold his muscular chest, and his arms were covered with tattoos. Even out of uniform, Jackie and her family knew him at once. This was the man who had carried Morales and Lerma back to the construction site on the day after the shooting and alerted Channel 32 to the scent of blood. Jackie remembered seeing that awful first news report, and how he had stood, smugly grinning behind DeAundria Keana Kelly. He was smiling now. And Pitt was smiling at him.

"Would you spell your name, please?" Pitt's voice was colorful and lilting, like a radio advertisement.

Book leaned back in his chair, as casually as he would have in his living room. "B-O-O-K. Clayton Book."

"And sir, by who are you employed?"

"Employed by the City of Ridgetop Police Department."

"Are you a POST-certified police officer?"

"I certainly am," Book crowed.

"And on Thursday, February 28, 2008, were you called out to the vicinity of Gideon Road and Old Betts Road?"

"I was."

"And why were you called out there?"

"I was dispatched in reference to copper thefts."

"And did you meet with anyone out there?"

"I met with Mr. Veitch." Jason dutifully raised his hand, as he had been instructed to do any time his name was mentioned. "The gentleman right over there, raising his hand."

"And when you met with the Defendant, what did you find?"

Jason lowered his hand. Except for Book and Pitt, the courtroom was deadly quiet. Book continued.

"We discussed how he was having difficulty completing any of his homes because of copper thefts."

"Did you and the Defendant, Mr. Veitch, discuss what to do about these copper thefts?"

Before Pitt had finished the question, Book answered, "We did."

"And tell us, Pitt continued, "what he had to say, the questions he asked, things he said."

"Well, he asked me how can we solve this issue, and I told him we frequently suggest that they install some type of surveillance cameras or the still deer cameras near the house."

"How did the Defendant respond to that?"

"Said he didn't like that idea; he intended to sit out and watch. See if he can catch them in the act."

Jason was nodding his head vigorously in protest and trying to say something to Kane. Jackie could hear a portion of Kane speaking to Jason, "...knew he would lie....expected it...let it go for now."

How could they let it go? How can this man be allowed to say any lie that comes into his head? Jackie looked to her right. The Hispanic community registered a range of emotions, from outrage, to satisfaction, to pain and loss. "We're all in this," thought Jackie, "We've all been wounded."

Pitt pushed onward, "Did he say he was planning on being armed?"

"Yes. Yes, he did."

"Did y'all talk about the concept of shooting these men?"

"We did. He asked if somebody showed up to steal his copper, was he justified in shooting the person."

"What did you respond to him?"

Book shrugged lightly, "Well, I told him no."

"And what was Mr. Veitch's reaction to that advice?"

"He was very upset that I told him he couldn't."

A rush of whispers swept through the courtroom at this remark. Kane was leaning toward Jason and speaking rapidly in his ear. Pitt took a moment to eye the jury significantly before she continued.

"Did you ever suggest to Mr. Veitch, as a remedy to these copper thefts, that he hire some teenagers to catch and beat up these perpetrators?"

"No. We never discussed anything at all about teenagers." Stephanie wheeled to Jackie, her eyes pained. They had been told to expect these blatant lies, but the reality of it was shocking and unnerving.

"Did you suggest to Mr. Veitch that he could make a citizen's arrest; that he could catch these guys, tie them to a post?"

"No, I did not."

"Did the two of you talk more about shooting?"

"When I told him he couldn't shoot them, he asked me, well, can I just shoot him in the leg. And I also explained to him, no, that he couldn't." When referencing Jason, Book appeared to have been speaking to a dim-witted child or a drug addled street thug.

Pitt was half-smiling in sympathy for the amount of time and effort Book apparently spent in trying to keep Jason from committing this terrible crime. She urged him on. "Can you describe his demeanor as y'all were talking and as the talk progressed?"

Book's voice was filled with ominous shadows now. "He was very upset. He was unusually determined to make apprehension of the subject. To be blunt. He was in a rage."

The jury was stilled with rapt attention. Their faces betrayed little, except for one man on the front row of the jury box. He wore a fearsome expression, his dark eyes unblinking, his face a map of unyielding coldness. Jackie shuddered and turned away.

Mitchell Kane appeared so very different from the first time the family had seen him. His handsome face and build were complimented by an immaculately tailored suit. Still, he had done little to gain the family's confidence. It was only due to Ellis's dogged recommendation that they kept him on the case. Kane walked up to the witness box, hesitated, and returned to his table, where he glanced at an open folder. Going back to the box, he finally spoke.

"It's *Officer* Book?"

"Yes."

"Fine."

"I'm *sorry*?" For no apparent reason, Book seemed to be offended.

"That's what I should call you, Officer Book?"

"You can call me Officer Book; Mr. Book."

"Why did you leave Crockett County Sheriff's Department?"

Book was silent.

"Mr. Book?"

"The official reason was unsatisfactory probationary period."

"Were you fired?"

"No. Terminated."

"Mr. Book, were you told as part of your termination that your ability to make good decisions and use good judgment was unsatisfactory?"

Book glared, but continued. "Yes, I was."

"Were you told that you continued to make bad decisions which resulted in bad circumstances?"

"Yes, I was."

"Were you told that you were insubordinate, with an insubordinate attitude toward supervisors?"

Kane had begun to fire his questions rapidly and Book answered just as sharply.

"Yes, I was."

"Were you told, Mr. Book, that you resort to intimidation to manipulate the outcome to your advantage?"

"Yes, I was."

"And that you damaged the reputation of both your coworkers and other agencies?"

Book was now sporting a deadly smile. "Yes, I was."

"And were you also told that you demonstrated a job performance which was unsatisfactory?"

"Yes, I was."

"And before you were with Crockett, you were with the City of Orlinda?"

"That is correct."

"And when you were up there, when there's a reprimand, it's called a personal contact?"

"That's correct."

"And you applied to the Crockett County Sheriff's Department after receiving three personal contacts in one week up in Orlinda, correct?"

"I don't think that's accurate."

"You don't?"

"No, I don't; I actually got a--"

Kane strode to his table and retrieved a thick folder. "Let me refresh you recollection, Mr. Book, and show you from your personnel file at the City of Orl--"

"Okay, so I don't know."

"Let me just show you a second one and see if that refreshes your recollect--"

"I told you I don't remember!" Book shot forward and spit this statement out with a fury that caused his voice to, literally, echo off the walls. Kane stood perfectly still and let the moment play itself out, and sink in to the spectators. Book's eyes eventually turned from Kane and wandered about the courtroom, then he once again leaned back in a pose that was exaggerated and casual.

"Now, Mr. Book, part of your training as a police officer is to write out reports when you respond to a complaint, correct?"

"That's correct."

"And in those reports you're supposed to put everything that's significant, correct?"

"*Pertinent* information."

"Pertinent. Now on February 28, you went out to Old Betts Road and you made a report. And your report at 3:51 has only two paragraphs, right?"

"That's correct."

"And nowhere in there did you say anything about his asking if he could shoot anybody, right?"

"That's correct."

"Nowhere in there did you say that he intended to go out there and stake it out himself?"

"That's correct."

"And nowhere in there did you state that he seemed unusually determined to apprehend these violators himself."

"That's correct."

Kane began to move slowly toward Book, his body suddenly animated; his speech rapid and sure. "So the fact that he seemed unusually determined to stop these men himself, intended to stake out the property himself, intended to carry weapons and seemed intent upon shooting someone -- none of this information seemed *pertinent*?"

"No."

"No?!"

"No, I-- No." Book's eyes darted uneasily for a moment, then settled back into their smug, heavy-lidded gaze.

"Mr. Book, were you at all concerned that if you had told Mr. Veitch to catch these people himself, that you might impose some liability on the sheriff's department?"

"Well, first I would never tell somebody that."

"Right, you would get in trouble if you were to tell somebody to go and arrest him yourself, right?"

Book thrust his head forward and spoke slowly again, as if to an idiot. "I would get in trouble if I were to tell somebody to take things into their own hands and then afterwards somebody were to get hurt from it."

Kane matched Book's slow, measured tone. "Well, in this case you did tell somebody to take it into their own hands, didn't you, and somebody did get hurt, didn't they?"

Book rose from his seat. "*How?* You tell me! You need to tell me exactly what you're referring to!"

Kane walked away and eyed the jury, leaving Book standing in the witness box. When Book had seated himself again, Kane returned to the questioning.

"Mr. Book, have you ever been called to the scene of burglaries or thefts in progress or drug deals or something of that nature?"

"Sure."

"And I know that police officers -- I commend you for a police officer. Y'all have a tough job. Whenever you go somewhere, you don't have any idea what's waiting for you, do you?"

"No. Always expect the unexpected."

"And you never know what might be waiting for you, if the person might be dangerous or armed, right?"

"We don't ever know what's waiting for us, Mr. Kane."

"When you do that, when you confront these people, do you draw your service weapon?"

"If there is a likelihood that somebody posed some type of immediate threat, yes --"

"You draw a weapon if you reasonably believe that there's a threat to you of being harmed?"

Book seemed bored with the questioning now. He tossed off his answer. "That's correct."

Kane paused and spoke in even tones. "So even a trained police officer will draw a weapon if he believes himself to be in danger?"

Book stared at Kane, but did not speak.

"Mr. Book?"

Still just Book's silent stare.

"Mr. Book?"

"You can call me *Officer* Book."

During the lunch break, Jackie picked at her salad, despite encouragement from the others. She knew she must keep up her strength and would eat later on. For now, she had no appetite. Each member of the family had something to say about the proceedings so far. Stephanie called Jennifer to see how J.J. was doing. Everyone wondered about Jason. They wished he could just eat lunch with them. Larry had asked if he could, if they promised not to talk about the case, or even had someone monitor them, but it was not allowed. They only saw him in the courtroom; mostly just the back of his head.

Upon returning from lunch, Jackie was glad she had not eaten. When Pitt called Dr. Jon Tod Coffelt, the medical examiner, she had demanded a large photograph of Juan Carlos Reymundo, laying on the stainless steel table in the morgue, be displayed for all to see. Jason felt the face of the corpse turned toward him, and thought that, at any moment, the eyes might open. He turned away. Jackie could not look away, and hardly grasped any of the medical jargon passing between Pitt and the ME, as she stared at the man's mutilated body. Stephanie kept her head down, but she listened.

With the photo still on display, Kane was now posing questions to Dr. Coffelt.

"Dr. Coffelt, in the autopsy report on the deceased Juan Carlos Reymundo, you made a description of -- if you will look on page three or four , you talked about the urinary system --"

"The *urogenital* system," Coffelt corrected.

"-- and that the urinary bladder is distended with urine. What does that mean?"

Coffelt's eyes narrowed warily. "That means he had a full bladder."

"And does the body continue to produce urine after a person is deceased?"

"No, of course not."

"From your experience, Dr. Coffelt, and what you know about the human body, would a person with a bladder distended in the manner that you reported, would that person be able to go to sleep?"

"That's hard to say."

"Okay, then, based on the condition of Mr. Reymundo's bladder, would you say it's more likely or less likely that this man had come onto a particular place and gone to sleep five minutes before?"

"I don't think I could say with certainty. I think it's difficult to say. I think. Well..."

Kane prodded him. "Dr. Coffelt?"

"Well, yes, I think it would be difficult for someone with this bladder in this condition to go to sleep."

"Thank you."

Stephanie could see Jason's face in profile and noticed a smile play on his lips. She understood this. In several of the reports that were read in the preliminary trial, both Lerma and Morales had stated that they -- as well as Reymundo -- were all fast asleep when Jason approached them. She was beginning to feel better about Kane.

Kane picked up a small wooden figure and placed it on the ledge of the witness box. It was an artist's model, jointed and representing the human body.

"Dr. Coffelt, will you agree, that according to the photos taken at the scene of the shooting, this model is in the exact position that the deceased was found?"

The doctor eyed him suspiciously, then offered, "Yes."

"Now, doctor, have you seen one of these artists' models before? It's just an articulated figure that you can move around. And if you would look at the back there, you can see there's a hole drilled, representing a bullet hole. And when a shotgun shoots, does it shoot in a straight line, particularly if it's a contact shot?"

"Yes."

"Now this hole was actually done by an engineer using your report. Does it appear to be an accurate representation of the wound?"

No response from Coffelt.

Kane restated. "Of the wound and its direction."

"Roughly . I'm not an expert on weaponry," the doctor offered grudgingly.

"But in order for a shotgun to have made this particular wound, that's the direction that the gun would have been pointed, correct?"

Again, no response.

"Dr. Coffelt--?"

"Yes."

Kane lifted a small, round stick. "So if I were to insert this object into the hole representing the wound, we would actually *see* the angle at which the bullet entered the body. And that does appear to be an accurate representation of the wound and its direction?"

"Yes."

"So, in the exact words of your report, Dr. Coffelt, that is a direct 35-to-40 degrees mild direction, leftward, approximately 10-to-20 degrees, correct?"

"That's correct."

"And I believe you have some familiarity with shotguns?"

"I am not an expert on weaponry, but I do know how a shotgun works."

"Then you must know that a 12-guage shotgun has a hefty kick and in order to fire it, you must place the stock against your shoulder in order to control the kick? Do you agree with that, Doctor?"

"Yes."

And with that, Kane slid the wooden stick into the hole drilled in the wooden model. It stuck straight up into the air.

"Oh, my, my!" Kane said in mock surprise. "It seems we have a problem here. Can you explain, Doctor, *barring his ability to fly*, can you explain how any human being could have been *shouldering* a shotgun and holding his hand on the trigger when it was fired at this angle?"

Once again, Coffelt did not answer. He just stared, puzzled, at the wooden model until Kane thanked him and walked away.

Jackie had bathed and washed her hair, drying it with a thick towel, then piling it on her head. Finding she was chilled, she pulled on slacks and a wooly, high-neck sweater. She wanted to bathe after her day in court, rather than wait 'til morning. She sent her red suit to the cleaners, although it was not soiled. Somehow, feeling so drained after the first day in court was welcome. Her body was limp and her mind would not focus. Cynthia dropped by to check on her. Larry left the two women to chat by the fire. Later, Jackie would have no memory of what was said. Suddenly, Cynthia was on the front steps, saying good night. Jackie leaned against the door frame, arms crossed. Cynthia turned back to her friend, looking so very tired, and spoke.

"Can I do anything for you before I go?"

"Tell me how to get through the night."

"Jackie, my precious, look for the lesson. Nothing leave us until the lesson is learned. So when the devil creep in tonight with his deep, dark thoughts, push him away by asking yourself: What am I to learn from all this? What is the lesson?"

Jackie let this sink in, and was silent for a moment, allowing her mind to find its way without force. "Be still and know that He is God. Listen. Listen. I think the lesson, for me, is to be still and listen."

Cynthia's smile lit the night. "Oh, I like that! Be still...and listen."

"But Cynthia. What if I say I can't do that?"

"It don't matter a bit. God says you can."

Cynthia leaned in and gave Jackie a hug, then silently walked down the stone steps to her car. Before she slid into the driver's seat, she turned and looked back at the house. Jackie stood silhouetted in the doorway, looking up at the deep night sky. "She is so very small," Cynthia thought, as she gathered her scarf against the damp, and drove away.

Jason sat up in bed. He had somehow learned to keep from screaming. The dreams were still touching him deep inside with a clammy grip that followed him out of sleep, but he had learned not to wake up screaming. He sat, wet and cold, hugging his knees and trying to control the shaking so that he did not wake Stephanie. How long before time to go back to court? Jason peered at the red numbers glowing on the digital clock. 12:56. That number seemed to have some significance. He was suddenly aware of a dripping sound. It was not coming from the bathroom, but much closer. It was just behind him; behind and slightly above, on the wall above the bed. This is where Stephanie had hung a beautiful painting of an old mill, taken from an actual location in the Black Forest of Germany. They both loved the greenish light that seemed to emanate from the trees and lend a glow to the stream and its mossy banks. And again, he heard the drip. Turning slowly, Jason looked up along the wall. There was the familiar, dark wood frame. And within it, the picture of Reymundo's body on the morgue slab. Jason told himself to be still until he found his way out of the maze of dreams; until he could really awaken. He hugged his knees closer and shook. But he did not scream.

CHAPTER NINE

MORALES FLINCHED. JUDGE CARROLL HAD SLAMMED HER gavel down when a fit of whispering broke out as Ernesto Morales took the stand. He could not seem to settle into the witness chair and his eyes darted about.

Pitt spoke to Morales very gently. "Tell us your name, please." Her brow was creased and she seemed to have great concern for him. Morales' curly hair was somewhat shorter than the last time Jackie's family had seen him, but he still wore the goatee. Today he was attired in a purple plaid shirt and jeans.

"Ernesto Morales," he answered in a soft voice, heavily accented.

"Can you spell that for the court reporter?"

"I can't."

"Where are you from?"

"Mexico."

"And how long have you been in this country?"

Morales hesitated. "Like, twelve years."

"And why did you come to this country?"

"To help my family and my parents."

"Did you learn a trade once you got here?" Pitt's voice was soft as she urged him on.

"Yes."

"And what trade is that?"

"Drywall."

"And do you work for Mister Darnell Grubbs of Grubbs' Drywall?"

"Yes."

"And do you have a crew?"

"Yes."

"And who is on that crew?"

"Jose Lerma and--" Morales' voice broke slightly. "-- and Juan Carlos Reymundo."

"And is that Jose Lerma seated over there -- raise your hand, please."

A silver-haired man leaned in and touched Lerma on the arm; he hesitated, then raised his hand.

"Yes," Morales answered quietly.

Pitt nodded sympathetically. "And Mr. Reymundo - is he the man who was murdered?"

In less than a heartbeat, Kane was on his feet, speaking even as he rose, "Objection, Your Honor!"

"Objection sustained." Judge Carroll swiveled her head toward Pitt and offered drily, "Ms. Pitt, you know better."

Pitt appeared to be deeply wounded and shocked at her carefully calculated slip. "My apologies, Your Honor, I will re-phrase. And is Mr. Juan Carlos Reymundo the man who was killed on the night of February 29, 2008?"

"Yes."

"And was he related to you?"

"Yes."

"And is Mr. Lerma related to you?"

"Yes, he is my cousin, too."

"Now, Mr. Morales, were you and your two cousins working on a house on Old Betts Road that is owned by Mr. Jason Veitch on February 29 of 2008?"

"Yes."

"And what time did you finish work on that day?"

"About ten o'clock at night."

"And what did you do then?"

"We going to the store, buy a lunch."

"And why is it that you went to the store to buy your lunch instead of returning to your homes to eat?"

"Because I want to stay on the job because I want to finish the houses, and I want to stay, you know, sleeping on the house for started working next day first thing in the morning."

"So where did you go to get something to eat?

"To a Wal-Mart."

"And after returning to the worksite, what did the three of you do?"

"I saw a car coming on the road."

Stephanie caught her breath. Morales was about to reveal that there had been a second man with Jason on that construction site. Her heart pounded. Stephanie knew where this would eventually lead.

"And where did this vehicle go?"

"It parked on the side of our van."

"And what did you do when you saw these lights coming up the road into the driveway and then by your van?"

"That it was the police."

"Thinking that, what did you next see or hear?"

Morales was gripping the arms of his chair tightly and staring fixedly at Pitt. "I heard when he shot his gun and he started yelling to get out of the van."

"And could you see this person?"

"I could just see that he was with a firearm."

"And was this the same person who was coming from the vehicle that pulled in behind you?"

"No," said Morales, "he was coming from the other direction."

"And what was this second man doing with his gun?"

"He was pointing at the van."

Pitt began to pick up speed, pushing Morales. "Was he saying anything?"

"Yes, to get out of the van."

"Did you get out of the van?"

"Yes."

"And what did you do after you got out of the van?"

"We got on the ground."

"And where were your hands?"

"Like this." Morales demonstrated by putting both hands behind his head. He inhaled sharply and the jurors could see tears fill his eyes.

Pitt looked to the jurors, then sympathetically to Morales before proceeding. "Did you or Mr. Lerma or Mr. Reymundo have any weapons on you?"

"No!"

"Did you or Mr. Lerma or Mr. Reymundo make any aggressive move toward the man?"

"No!" Morales' voice broke into a sob.

Pitt picked up her pace again. "The person with the gun that was standing there in front of you telling you to get out of the van, to get on the ground, is he the Defendant here on trial?"

"Yes!"

"When you got out of the van, did you say anything to him?"

"Yes, I am asking, I'm just working here. I'm working for Grubbs' Drywall."

"When you said that, what, if anything, did he say or do?"

"He would just say to shut up and put our hands behind our heads."

"When you three were laying on the ground, " Pitt moved in close, "were there any lights on you?"

"Yes, the driver that drive up behind us, he was putting some flashlight at us, but that was all the lights."

"What was the Defendant doing while all three of you were on the ground?"

"Not to move and to shut up and not to look at him."

"Were you afraid?" Pitt asked, her voice heavy with pity.

Morales' voice was very small when he managed to say, "Yes."

Gently, "Then what happened?"

After a moment, Morales wiped his nose on his sleeve and answered, "I heard a shot."

"Was anybody shot?"

"Juan Carlos."

Here Pitt paused for full effect, looked at the jurors once again, then back to Morales before asking, "And after Juan Carlos Reymundo was shot, did he say anything to you?"

Morales managed to choke out, "Cousin," before he pitched his head forward and began to sob.

Jackie turned away from the sight. Though this man's testimony was geared to take her son away, she could not help but be affected by his pain. He seemed confused and frightened and genuinely heartbroken. Her gaze was drawn across the aisle to a tiny woman in a worn brown dress and sweater. The woman held something in her hand. She was gently and lovingly wiping a picture frame, which held a photograph of a young man, with a crumpled handkerchief. After a moment, Jackie could see that his face was dressed in a broad smile. And suddenly Jackie recognized the face, which she had seen looking very different, on a mortician's slab. This was a photograph of Juan Carlos Reymundo, perhaps his high school graduation picture. And the woman tending to the picture, was his mother. Jackie clutched her Bible close, in both hands.

Drawn toward the jury box, Jackie's eyes rested on the jurors. All eyes were on Pitt and Morales, except for one. The juror with the cold dark eyes, the man on the front row who had caused Jackie to shudder on the first day of trial, was looking directly at Jackie. He did not blink. She turned away, and held her Bible closer.

Pitt continued to question a distraught Morales. "After you realized your cousin was shot, what did you say or do?"

"I'm asking help please because call 911 and call the police. I'm just working here."

"And what, if anything, did the man with the gun say or do?"

"He kept pointing the gun at us and told us not to move and don't look at him."

"Had you tried to move before Juan Carlos Reymundo was shot?"

"No, because I was scared."

"Had Juan Carlos tried to move?"

"No," he gulped.

"After Juan Carlos Reymundo was shot, did you attempt to move or make any aggressive move toward the Defendant?"

"No!"

"And what, if anything, did the Defendant do then?"

"He asked the driver that was there in the vehicle and asked him to put him in the vehicle and to take him to the hospital."

"Did someone pick up Juan Carlos?"

"The one with the flashlight and asked him if he could walk."

"How did that man get Juan Carlos Reymundo to his truck?"

"He just pick him up from behind and like dragged him."

Jackie and Larry listened, aghast, and held each other tightly. Stephanie turned and gazed across the aisle and saw expressions of shock and disgust. One man shook his head slowly as tears rolled down his cheeks.

Pitt walked over to the jury box, as if to speak. Then, seeming to be overcome with emotion, she drew her hand to her mouth, and walked away. The cold-eyed man in the jury turned his gaze from Morales and stared at Jackie and her family.

Mitchell Kane handed a clean handkerchief to Ernesto Morales. He retrieved it with thin, dark fingers and wiped his eyes and nose.

"Mr. Morales, I know this is difficult for you, and I'm going to be as easy as I can. Will you just answer a few questions for me?"

"That's okay."

"Now on the evening of February 29, 2008, I believe you said you stopped working about 10 o'clock that night."

"Yes."

"And then -- help me out a little bit. You were questioned by the sheriff, after this incident, down at the sheriff's department?"

"Yes." Morales folded the handkerchief into a small square and placed it in his pocket.

"And you were in a little room, and they were videotaping it. Did you know that they were videotaping it?" Kane was speaking clearly, making certain Morales understood each word and phrase.

"Yes."

"And did you tell the sheriff's deputy at that time that you left about 8 o'clock or 8 thirty to go get something to eat?"

Morales shook his head. "No."

"So you told them on the videotape that it was 10 o'clock?"

"Yes."

Kane stopped, turned and looked directly at the jury for a moment. Then he returned to questioning Morales.

"Mr. Morales, when you returned from eating at Wal-Mart on the night of February 29, did you return directly to the driveway of the house on Old Betts Road?"

"Yes."

"Didn't you go down Gideon Road, pass by Old Betts Road, and go to the end of Gideon Road?"

"No."

"Did you then not turn around and go back down Gideon Road, passing by Old Betts Road a second time?" Kane was still not confrontational, but rather explaining each point and question slowly and clearly.

"No!"

"So you drove directly to the house?"

"Yes."

"And when you gave your recorded statement, did you tell the officer that you had forgotten where it was and you turned the wrong way?"

"I didn't say that."

"If we could lower the lights, I'm going to play a portion of your statement for you."

One deputy quickly wheeled in a large monitor while another flipped a bank of light switches in the back of the courtroom. On the screen appeared Morales, still in his muddy clothing on the night of the shooting. He was seated at a small table in a single pool of light. With his back to the camera, an officer stood, asking Morales questions. Morales was caught mid-sentence.

"...we leave about 8 or 8:30 to get something to eat."

"Where did you go to eat?" asked the officer

"Arby's."

"And when you came back to the house after eating, did you come directly to the house?"

"No, we drive around and around."

"And, Mr. Morales, why did you do that?"

"We are talking a lot and it's, like, real dark, and so we drive too far and then go up, like to where you can turn around, and then come back and drive real slow but we don't find the road."

"So what do you do when you can't find Old Betts Road?"

"We turn around again, and then we come to a stop sign, and that's where we turn off the van."

"And what did you do after you turned off the engine?"

"We turn off the lights and try to go to sleep."

"And did you go to sleep?"

"No, because, in a minute we can see better in the dark and we see and we start up again and we go to the house."

"So you couldn't find the house because it was dark."

"Yeah, so that's why we drive around and around."

The officer summed up Morales explanation neatly, repeating slowly for his approval. "So, let me get this straight. You passed by Old Betts and went to the end of Gideon, where you turned around, then you drove slowly down Gideon, but passed by Old Betts again. So you turned around again, came to the stop sign at Old Betts where you turned off the engine and lights. In a few minutes, you started up the vehicle again and pulled into the drive at the house on Old Betts, is that right?"

Morales answered, "Yes," and nodded in full agreement.

Kane asked for the lights to be brought back up. Stephanie, wide-eyed and grinning, turned to Jim, who was smiling broadly. Ellis, trying to hide his pleasure, nonetheless nodded his head in satisfaction. It appeared as if they had just won the case. How could they convict anyone on the basis of such wildly conflicting testimony? And not hearsay, the entire courtroom had just witnessed it!

Kane walked up to Morales and rested his hands on the witness box. "Mr. Morales, is your recollection refreshed now that you have heard what you told the deputy?"

"Yes, we like, turn right and then turn left and then turn the wrong way."

"Mr. Morales, are you aware that many, many things you are telling us today are completely different from the things that you told the police in your videotaped interview?"

Morales tossed off his response lightly. "Yes, but it's hard to remember everything. I remember some things but not everything."

Kane strolled easily to the jury box, paused, but said not a word. Then he looked evenly at the spectators, then directly into Pitt's eyes as he said, "I have no more questions, Your Honor."

Larry and Jackie sat in their SUV during the lunch break. It was the only place they could find any degree of privacy. Larry watched the trees and sky, eyes slightly squinted as if looking for something in particular. Jackie rested her elbow in the open window and her cheek in her hand. After a moment she spoke thoughtfully.

"Larry, I want to go see Jason tonight."

"All righty."

"This could be his last night at home. We never know."

"Could be."

"What if they finish up tomorrow and the verdict comes in and this is his last night at home?"

"Um-hm."

"They won't let us talk to him in court; am I supposed to give up this last night, too?"

"Dunno."

Jackie sighed and rested her hand on her Bible. Silence.

"I can't take his last night, can I?"

Larry, silent.

"If it is his last night of freedom, he needs to be with Stephanie and J.J., doesn't he?"

"Hmmm."

"And I need to give him that, don't I?"

"Umph."

"I need to let them have their time together."

Larry, silent.

"You're right. Thank you for talking me out of that."

"Yep."

"You always know the right things to say."

Larry smiled just a little, then went back to watching the sky.

Judge Carroll turned and addressed Evelyn Pitt. "Do you have another witness to call?"

Pitt stood, smoothed the skirt of her navy suit, and replied, "I do, Your Honor. I call Bill Flournoy."

Stephanie grabbed a sharp breath and reached for Jim's hand. She understood this moment was coming. Only a handful of people knew that her father had been on the construction site on that terrible night. Bill Flournoy was a gentle and honest man. He lived simply and privately, enjoying the companionship of his family and close friends. And this entire ordeal had taken a terrible toll on him. Stephanie had only recently learned that Pitt had visited her father and led him to believe that, if he did not testify, he would be jailed for contempt, and possibly as an accessory to murder. But that was not why he had forced himself to go through this torturous appearance. He was doing it for his family. He was doing it for Jason.

Billy walked into the courtroom in jeans and workboots, but he had put on a good jacket and carefully combed his hair. It was clear from his entrance that he was uneasy and unsure. A deputy aimed him toward the witness box. He mounted it, started to sit, then corrected himself and stood, waiting with his right hand raised. Pitt rapidly swore him in, then directed him to sit.

"Have a seat, sir, and please tell us your name."

"Billy Flournoy."

"Mr. Flournoy, you live here in Crockett County?"

"Yes, ma'am."

"All your life?"

"All my life."

"And are you related to Jason Veitch, the Defendant on trial?"

"I'm his father-in-law."

"And that makes him married to your daughter?"

"Right. Stephanie."

Stephanie was so proud of her daddy; he was doing very well.

"And do you work for your son-in-law?"

"Yes, ma'am. For most of eight years now."

"And what kind of work do you do for him?"

"Well, I'm sort of like a handyman on his houses."

"And were you aware of some copper thefts on these houses about this time last year?"

Billy continued to answer in his dry, direct manner. "Yes, ma'am."

"And what was Jason Veitch's reaction to his houses getting hit by these copper thieves?"

"Well, ma'am, he didn't like it."

The courtroom erupted into guffaws. Stephanie knew this was just her daddy's unadorned speech, but to the spectators, it sounded like a perfectly timed comic zinger.

Pitt's eyes grew narrow, then she showed the courtroom a charming smile before turning back to Billy.

"Let me put this in a language you can understand." Then very slowly, as if to a child, "Did he express a reaction?"

Billy made a real attempt to make himself understood. "Every time one was hit, he had to have the stuff replaced, and it was costing him a good bit of money."

"Did you know that Jason Veitch was going to go out to Old Betts Road Friday night, February 28?"

"Well, yes'm, but I believe it was February the 29th."

Again, a ripple of laughter at Pitt's expense. She smiled.

"Did you know he was going to go out to Old Betts Road Friday night, February the *29th*?"

"Yes, ma'am."

"What did he tell you he was going to do?"

"He just said he was going to go out and see if he could help the law catch who's been stealing."

"Did you talk with Jason Veitch any time on February 29 on the phone?"

"Yes, he called me during the night. It was, you know, it was after midnight."

"And when he called you after midnight, what did he say?"

"He told me that he was being robbed out on lot three. And I asked him, I said have you called the law. He said yes. And I asked him did he want me to come over there, and he said yes."

"And did you go over there?"

"Yes."

"So when you got to Gideon and Old Betts Road, tell us what you saw."

Billy took a ragged breath and wiped the palms of his hands on his jeans. For the first time, he took his eyes off Pitt and focused on what he had seen the night of the 29th.

"All I saw was a white van."

"And when you saw that van, what did you do?"

"I pulled up sorta close to the van."

"And then you got out and stood by the driver's door?"

"Right."

"And you had a flashlight."

"Right."

"And what did you do with the flashlight?"

"I started shining it at the van."

"Why were you shining it at the van?"

"I just wanted to see if there was somebody in it, you know."

"What's the next thing that happened?"

Billy's forehead reflected with a fine sheen of sweat. "Okay, well, it wasn't long that I heard a shot."

"Close? Far?"

"It was pretty close over in them woods to the left there."

"After you heard the gun go off, then what happened?"

"Okay, just a few seconds it seemed like I saw Jason walk up."

"And what was he doing when you first saw him?"

"He had his gun and it was aimed up high."

"Was he saying anything?"

"He come up," Billy stammered, then recovered, "He come up, like I say, at the van and he started to order them out of the van."

"Then what happened?"

"After some time, they started coming out of the van."

"How many came out?"

"Two."

"And what happened after the two got out of the van?"

"Well, things started getting tense because we could hear somebody rustling around in the van, and they wouldn't come out."

"So when these two guys got out, did they make an aggressive action toward you?"

"No."

"Did they make any aggressive action toward your son-in-law?"

"Not that I recall."

"Were you in fear of your safety from these two guys?"

"Yes. Yes."

"And tell us about that. Why were you in fear of these two frightened, unarmed men?"

"Just the fact that I didn't know who they was out there in the middle of the night. I didn't know if they had weapons."

"Did you *see* any weapons?"

"No, but I could tell there was more inside."

"Did he eventually come out?"

"Yes."

"And when he came out, what did he do?"

"He wasn't as calm as the other two."

"Did he make an aggressive move toward you?"

"He was like," Billy's voice shook, "he was looking around like, you know. He wanted to do something, either run or, you know."

"So you were in fear of this unarmed man because he was looking around." Pitt paused to send a conspiratorial smile toward the jury box. "Now the first two, were they on the ground at some point?"

"At some point, yes."

"Did the third one get on the ground?"

"Eventually he did."

"And where were their hands while they were on the ground?"

"Well, the first two, they was behind their back, like this." Billy stood and locked his hands behind his lower back, very different from the pose demonstrated by Morales. "But the third one, no he didn't want to do that."

"And what happened when he didn't want to do that?"

"He would get down, then he would get back up, and, you know, look around and stuff like that."

"So what happened then?"

102

"He was trying to get up at one time there, and Jason pushed him down easy with his foot there on his shoulder."

"And when he pushed the third guy down on the ground with his foot, what happened next?"

Billy grabbed a breath and plowed on. "This guy, everybody was trying to get him to put his hands behind his back and he wouldn't do it. And I went up to him, and I tapped him on the hand to make him understand that you need to put your hands behind your back."

"And so what did you do after hitting him on the hand?"

"Well, I about done decided this guy wasn't going to put his hands behind his back. Cause his buddies told him over and over in Mexican that's what he should do, but he wouldn't mind them neither. He was still active, like he wanted to do something. So I started back toward my truck to get some rope."

"And that seemed to you the most reasonable thing to do at the time?"

"Yes, ma'am, it did."

"And why is that?"

"Well, ma'am, we still didn't know if they might be more in the van or maybe in the house."

"And so what happened then?"

Billy was tense and on edge, and it showed in his posture and voice. He had just described the echoing crack of a gunshot, and the awful screams that followed. Mitchell Kane led him firmly onward.

"...and, Mr. Flournoy, you said that everybody was in shock, right?"

"Yessir."

"Did Jason appear to be in shock?"

"Yes."

"Is there any question in your mind that this shooting might have been intentional?"

"No, Mr. Kane, it was not intentional. I can tell you that."

"And you've known Jason for how long?"

"I've known him about nine years."

"Is he a hothead?"

"No."

"Does he get angry?"

"No."

"Have you ever seen him raise his voice?"

"Never."

"Have you ever heard him use a curse word?"

"Not ever."

"Church-going man?"

"Yessir."

"Ever been in trouble?"

"Not ever."

"Is he a vigilante type that wants to go out and get revenge on somebody for taking his property?"

"No."

"You told him when he asked you what do I do now, you said, 'Jason, just tell the truth.'"

"Just tell the truth," Billy replied simply.

"And has he always told the truth about how this happened?"

"Yes."

"And has he always said the same thing?"

"Yes."

"It's always been what you described?"

"Always the truth."

"Thank you, Mr. Flournoy."

Stephanie allowed herself a tiny smile. She sure loved her daddy.

Larry pulled out of the parking deck. They managed to miss the bulk of the crowd today. No press around this area. Suddenly Jackie asked him to pull over. Billy was walking down the sidewalk. Upon recognizing their vehicle sliding up beside him, Billy stopped and stuck his head in the window. Jackie looked at his sweet, tired eyes.

"Billy, are you alright?"

"Just fine as frog hair, Miz Jackie."

"I want to thank you for all you've done; for all you did today. I know that wasn't easy."

"Well, I didn't do nothing, really. Just told the truth."

"That was enough. That's everything. The truth."

Jackie reached out the door and gently patted Billy on his cheek. Then they went their separate ways.

Daylight was fading, but store lights and windows illuminated the sidewalk on the town square. Jason had a big day tomorrow and a big decision to make, but he could not rest. And so they walked.

"Mr. Kane says the most dangerous thing I can do is to take the stand."

"That's what he says," Stephanie agreed.

"But then he says I have to take the stand if I'm to have even a chance of acquittal."

"Yes, Jason."

"So, which one am I supposed to do?" Jason persisted.

Stephanie paused before a store window filled with kid mannequins dressed in spring outfits. She could imagine J.J. wearing the little blue striped suit. Maybe someday they could have a little girl to dress in yellow and pink. If only... Stephanie took her husband's hands in hers.

"Don't you believe God knows whether you should take the stand or not?"

Jason looked into Steph's eyes and answered, "I do." Then turning away, "Think He'll let me know?"

Heading on down the sidewalk, Jason seemed defeated. "I'm still in jail. Trapped. Steph, I'm just lost."

Stephanie caught up with her husband and held his hand. They walked for a moment before she spoke again.

"My daddy always says just because you don't know where you are, doesn't mean you're lost."

"Honey, I have no idea what that means."

"Neither do I." The last light of day slipped away, as, hand in hand, they walked on.

CHAPTER TEN

TRIAL - DAY THREE

ONE RAP OF THE GAVEL. THAT'S ALL IT TOOK TO GET THE ATTENtion of everyone in the courtroom. Judge Carroll said little. Her face remained impassive. But when she spoke, her words were delivered with such commanding simplicity that she owned the room. She returned her gavel to its resting place and spoke in deep and resonant tones.

"From here on out, I hope I don't have to repeat myself. During cross-examination by counsel, a question was asked whether or not the gentleman was shot on purpose. And I heard from this area over here, I heard someone say the word: 'Yes.' That needs never happen again in this courtroom. If I hear one more comment of this type, I will clear this side of the courtroom. You may proceed."

Mitchell Kane turned his attention from the judge back to the witness stand. Jason Veitch sat, appearing composed, and performing better than Kane had ever imagined. Putting Jason on the stand was a dangerous and deadly gamble; Kane never willingly placed the Defendant on the stand if it could be helped. But he felt that, if Jason could keep his focus and reveal his honesty to the jurors, that this might be his path to freedom. Jason appeared poised but sincere. Good. Passion and ferocity would have worked against him. On the few occasions when Jason began to elaborate unnecessarily, Kane led him back with a simple, "That's not what I asked you." So far, things were looking up.

For Jackie, this was harder than she could have imagined. To see her son reliving this incident was almost unbearable. For Stephanie, it was gut-wrenching for a totally different reason: She had been in on the counseling sessions with Kane, and knew that with one slip, Jason could send himself to prison. J.J. would be thirty-seven years old when Jason was released.

Kane resumed his questioning about the advice Jason had been given. "When you mentioned the bad points about the use of deer cameras to Deputy Book, what did he say?"

"He says, 'Well, why don't you just hire a group of teenage guys to come out here, and when they come to steal the copper, just beat them up.' And I said, 'What am I going to do if these people that's robbing these houses have guns and shoots one of these teenage boys? Then I'm going to feel like this whole thing is my fault.' And I told him that."

This was good, the simple truth from Jason. Kane proceeded, "So, armed with your gun for protection, your cell phone for communication, and a flashlight, you seated yourself on a plastic bucket in the woods and began to watch, around 10:30 on Friday night."

"Yes, sir."

"Jason, how do you know it was around that time?"

"I called my mom as soon as I got there and that was at 10:24."

Kane knew this was the wrong response and tried again. "How do you know it was exactly 10:24?"

"From my cell phone records."

This was the correct answer. Kane wanted Jason to be as precise and factual as possible. They were all about to enter the woods and things would likely become emotional. It was Kane's job to guide Jason - and the jury - through this dark night in question.

"Jason, did you have any other incoming or outgoing calls?"

"A few. I called Steph - Stephanie a couple of times and Billy, but mostly I just waited."

"What was it like out there, Jason?"

Jason paused and looked at his hands, folded in his lap. "It was just very dark and very quiet."

"Any cars out there?"

"I don't recollect a single car," Jason responded in his soft Georgia drawl.

"Did you see anything at all?" Kane moved in, placing a hand on the witness stand. "Anything to get your attention?"

"Nothing got my attention until I saw a car coming off in the distance some time after midnight."

"Okay. Kane stepped back, not wanting to obscure the courtroom's view of Jason. "Tell us about that."

"I didn't know if it was a car or truck; I just saw headlights coming up real slow. It came down Gideon Road and when it came to the stop sign at Old Betts Road, it went straight through. Then there's this little turn-around area down there where they're building another subdivision and it pulled in there and it backed out and headed back my way, real slow." Jason's eyes were fixed on some distant memory; he seemed to have lost touch with his immediate surroundings. "I was shakin' and just hopin' it would keep on going. But when it got back to the stop sign, it kind of pulled off on the side and stopped. And it turned its lights off."

Softly, Kane asked, "What happened then?"

"It just sat there and then it crunk back up and the lights come back on and then it come real slow down Old Betts Road and then it turned into my driveway. When it did, the lights shined right on me, and I just dove into the woods."

The plastic bucket he'd been sitting on flipped over with a plunking sound as Jason dove into the bed of pine needles and briars. He had no idea whether he'd been seen. The woods initially seemed to be good cover, but when the glare of the headlights swept past, he realized how bare February had left the trees.

Suddenly, darkness, as the headlights were cut. Then silence as the engine was cut. Jason could make out the ghost of a white van, sitting still in the gravel driveway. Nothing more happened for an eternity. Then, hands shaking violently, he propped himself up on elbows and attempted to call 911, while using his body to block off as much of the cell phone's light as possible. One try, then a second, and finally on the third he heard the ring. A dispassionate female voice crawled into his ear.

"Crockett County 911 Operator #712. What is your emergency?"

"Yes..." Jason's voice seemed high and loud and he struggled to hold it steady. "Gideon Road and Old Betts Road in Ridgetop."

"I'm sorry, sir, say that again? Sir?"

"Gideon Road and Old Betts Road in Ridgetop."

"What is your address?"

Why couldn't she just help him? Jason tried to steady his hand, but his entire body was shaking. He couldn't seem to keep the phone's light hidden. Absurdly, he though there must be a way to turn off the light; he should know that. Why didn't he know how? "It's a new house. I'm hiding in the woods. I'm being robbed."

The operator sighed, indicating clearly that Jason was inconveniencing her. "All right, hold on; let me transfer you to the sheriff's office. Stay on the line with me."

This could not be happening. There were officers nearby, Deputy Book had promised. Why wouldn't she just notify them? The phone rang and rang, occasionally punctuated by the operator's demand that Jason stay on the line.

"Sheriff's office."

The 911 operator began to chat easily with the sheriff's operator, as if Jason were not even hearing, or in danger. "I have a caller for you," she began, "that says he's at Gideon Road and Old Betts Road in Ridgetop. He's hiding in the woods and he says he's being robbed."

"What's your address?" demanded the second woman. Jason was unsure if she meant he was to keep repeating the address. Surely not. Then, "*Sir,* what's your address?"

"It's a brand new house; I don't have that address. I can't talk."

Undaunted, the woman from the sheriff's office continued, "And it's being robbed?"

"Yes!"

"What's your name."

Near tears, "I can't talk."

"Okay, but you're in the woods at Gideon Road and Old Betts Road?"

"Yes!"

"Well. Okay. How are we going to find you - will you come out when we send a deputy, or...?"

Jason heard himself say, "I'm willing to bet I'm the only person hiding in the woods at this address," but it was only in his mind. To the operator, "Yes."

"Okay. Can you stay on the phone with me?"

"I can't. And I can't talk. I gotta hang up."

At this point the operators began chatting between themselves again. One of them commented, "Hey 911, do you have his phone number? Cause this sounds kinda...."

"Yeah, I do have his phone number."

Jason had the presence of mind to say clearly, "Don't call me back," before he disconnected. He would try to find the button to mute the ring. Why hadn't he learned where that button was?

In total darkness now, Jason felt solitary and helpless. He couldn't leave. But if he stayed....they could be coming toward him even now. He could see almost nothing. The van, a vague milky glow in the distance was the only image his eyes could acquire. He reassured himself that Book had promised cars would be in the area. Surely they would be making random passes. Surely the operators, despite their skepticism, would have contacted them by now. Jason began to realize that the light from his phone had caused his irises to contract. Maybe if he waited a bit, he could see better. See what? He wanted to check his watch, but it had a lighted dial. In order to see the time, he'd have to activate it. How much time had passed since his call? Something cracked behind him. Had they gone down the road and circled up behind him? No, he would have seen the interior lights of the van when they opened the door and heard the door shut. Unless they had no interior light. And maybe they opened the door silently, exited, and left the door open. Jason could no longer tell if he was actually hearing his heart beat or could merely feel the pounding in his head. He missed the operators. This waiting, alone, in darkness, was almost more than he could bear. He imagined something was moving in the bed of pine straw beneath his chest and was grateful for the heavy jacket he wore.

Maybe he should try to turn off the ringer on his phone. He lifted it to his face, but saw nothing. Cradling the phone to cover the light, Jason dialed instead. The ring was comforting and soon he heard Billy's muffled voice.

"Billy, it's Jason. They're here--"

"Hello?"

"Jason. Jason."

"Jason?"

"Billy, they're here. They're out here now. I'm being robbed."

Billy's voice was sharp now. "Did you call the law?"

"Billy, I can't talk. Listen. I'm out here in the woods and I don't know if they can see me. I called 911. They should have the police here any second now."

"Jason, you want me to come out there?"

"Lot three. Police said they'd have somebody patrolling the area all night. They'll be right here. You come on when you can. Don't tell Mom or Steph. I'm gonna hang up now. Don't call back."

Jason looked at the time before he disconnected. 12:49. He closed the phone and realized he felt somewhat better. The police had to be here in seconds. They'd had plenty of time to call the squad cars and get them here, even if they were as far as a mile or two away. He squinted for approaching lights in the distance. After it was all settled, it would be good to have Billy here to steady him and make the calls to Steph and Jim and Larry and Jackie.

Jason waited. He thought he heard the sound of a car in the distance, but then there was only silence. Which way would they come from? He craned his head around. And waited. Why weren't they here? This didn't make any sense. He'd called 911 some time ago. And Book had promised...promised....

Suddenly the edges of the trees were illuminated. The police were here! He could see the van more clearly now; even make out the ladder secured to the top. Jason stretched his head to see which direction the police cruiser was coming from, but could not find their headlights. Then a breeze shivered the trees. He looked up at the night sky. Oh, no. It was the moon. The night wind had brushed away the clouds and the moonlight had lit the wood. No police. Jason checked his watch again. 12:56. It had been seven minutes since he ended his call to Billy. Seven minutes, plus maybe six on the phone to 911 and he knew for sure it was at least five between calls and yet the police ---

And there it was! No mistake now. Coming from behind him down Old Betts Road and cutting through the woods with its headlights was the police car! The vehicle slowed as it came to the makeshift drive leading to the half-finished house and then crunched into the gravel. He looked hard at the van as the headlights illuminated it, but could make out no one inside. Then the engine was cut. He turned his eyes to the vehicle, still with headlights on high beam. Strangely, they had sent a truck instead of a regular police car. A red truck. Billy's red Ford Ranger.

"Oh, Lord, please; Billy, no!"

It had never occurred to Jason that the police would not come to help him. Billy had arrived on the site and exited his truck and was walking toward the van.

"Billy, please stay back!" Jason whispered to himself.

Aiming his flashlight at the driver's window, Billy shouted, "All right, now; I want ya'll to come on out now." He just stood, holding the flashlight on the van, until the shotgun blast caused him to jump. Billy turned toward the dark woods just in time to see Jason charge out, shotgun held high and pointed skyward.

"The police are on their way and I got a gun; ya'll need to step out of there right now!" Jason's voice was adrenalin-fueled by the act of firing a gun for the first time in his life.

Billy and Jason looked at one another, then at the van. Nothing moved. Billy kept his flashlight relatively steady on the driver's window. Still, they could see nothing inside. Windows must be tinted. After a long moment, the door opened and a figure emerged.

"Put your hands up, now; up, up," Jason barked as command-ingly as he could, "police are on their way."

Ernesto Morales put his hands high in the air. Jose Lerma slid out of the driver's door next, and looking at Morales, raised his hands as well. Both were speaking softly, but neither Billy nor Jason understood Spanish. Jason just wanted them to keep their hands in sight, away from any possible weapons. They would stay here all night, if necessary. Someone would eventually come to help. Suddenly the van rocked slightly.

"Hey, they's more in there!" shouted Billy, stepping away from the vehicle. At the same instant, both Morales and Lerma lowered their hands and began to shout.

Jason had to bellow in order to be heard over the three men and ordered, "Y'all lay down on the ground now. Both of you. Down on the ground right here." He had the presence of mind to gesture clearly, and reluctantly they sank to their knees, then lay, face-down, on the ground.

A noise from inside the van made both Billy and Jason jump, as their eyes darted between the van and the two men on the ground.

"Behind your back, behind your back," Jason shouted and gestured to the two men. "Put your hands behind your back!"

Billy leaned in, slapped the back of the van with his hands, and shouted, "Come on out, now; we can hear you in there," before stepping back and aiming his flashlight at the double back doors of the dirty vehicle. It was impossible to see in the back windows either. Despite Jason's best efforts, the two men on the ground continued shouting; he wondered if they were urging the occupants of the van to exit or to fire upon him and his father-in-law. Suddenly the back door flew open.

Juan Carlos Reymundo jumped from the van and hit the ground shouting and gesturing wildly. His voice was ferocious and his words spewed non-stop, as he waved, lunged, and pounded the side of the van with his fist. Morales and Lerma added to the confusion by continuing to shout at him, and Billy and Jason's attempts to get their attention only added to the chaos. Jason could see that Billy was too close to this large, agitated man and could be struck or attacked at any second. The man's hands continuously disappeared behind his back and into his open coat and Jason expected to see them emerge with a weapon any time. He shouted at Billy to stay back, but didn't seem to be heard above the din.

Finally, they were able to coax Reymundo near his companions and he sank to his knees, but then jumped up again abruptly. His arms were out, then over his head, then he would lunge at Billy or Jason. The men on the ground continued shouting and yelling orders and Reymundo had turned on them, angrily, more than once. And so it continued, Jason white with fear as the big man got to his knees, then sprang up, went halfway to the ground then lunged at them again. Finally he was in the same pushup position as the other two, but seemed adamant about not putting his hands behind his back. Jason moved close and attempted to urge him to stay down by pushing his shoulder gently to the ground, but this just caused him to spring up again. Back down on the ground now, but pounding it with his fists to punctuate his shouts, he received a light tap on one arm from Billy's flashlight; Billy was attempting to show him that he needed to put his arms behind his back. Reymundo jumped and lunged at Billy, a dangerous hulk of a man in the truck headlights.

"Billy, get back!" Jason cried. "Just get back!" Billy headed toward his truck. Jason moved in to Reymundo and gestured with the shotgun, which he held by the stock. Terrified and at the end of his rope, Jason used the gun to push the man down. When he was finally face down, Jason turned away. Reymundo reached out in less than a heartbeat and grabbed Jason by the cuff of his pants, throwing him off balance. Jason half-wheeled and shouted, "Stay down, stay down!" as he used the shotgun to push him to the ground. Gripping the stock, he pushed Reymundo to the ground once, then again.

Billy felt the gun blast and saw the trees before him light up, as if someone had taken a flash picture. He turned slowly and saw dark fluid running down the side of the van. Then the silent few seconds were broken by screams from the men on the ground. They seemed to be begging or praying, he couldn't tell. He just knew they were screaming.

Jason walked to Billy in slow motion, the shotgun, still held by the stock, dragging the ground.

"Billy. I did not mean to do that. Billy. What am I going to do?"

Billy's voice was steady. "Just tell the truth."

"Billy, you're right. The truth; just tell the truth," Jason murmured as he dialed 911. He lifted the phone to his ear and noticed how odd and thin his voice sounded as he spoke. "Send an ambulance--send an ambulance to the corner of Gideon Road and Old Betts Road. Someone's been shot--"

Someone was softly repeating, "Jason. Jason?" It was Kane, drawing Jason's attention back to the courtroom. So many people were crying all about, but he was not aware of them. Finally, he heard his own voice again. "Everything was kind of -- I was -- they told me to apply some pressure to the wound, so that's what I was trying to do."

"Okay, Jason, did the ambulance come?"

"No, sir."

"Did the police come?"

"No, sir."

"So what did you do?"

"Billy said we need to get this man to the hospital and I said, 'you're right,' and so we picked him up and put him in Billy's truck"

"How did you pick him up?"

"One arm was around Billy and one arm was around me. We just walked him over there."

"You didn't drag him or--"

"No, sir; we picked him up and carried him all the way."

"Jason, were you not concerned about getting his blood on you?"

"I wanted Mr. Reymundo to live."

"Pardon?"

"I wasn't worried about blood. I just wanted him to live."

The look on Evelyn Pitt's face was hard to describe. She paced about before the witness box, glancing at Jason with -- disgust? amusement? disbelief? Each time she looked at the jurors, she seemed about to raise her hands heavenward, as if to say, "Do you believe the bull this man is throwing at you?" Yet always, she retained her poise, dignity, and sweet smile. Her shoes complimented her pale blue suit beautifully and her jewelry was tastefully understated.

"Isn't it true, Mr. Veitch, that the single thought you had on your mind was that if anybody came out to rob any of your houses, they weren't going to get away with it; isn't that true?"

"No, ma'am. All I wanted was for the police to catch whoever was doing this."

"And you ignored Deputy Clayton Book's advice that if you saw somebody out there to call 911, didn't you?"

"No, ma'am, I called 911 just like Deputy Book said, but he didn't have any officers in the area, like he told me he would. And I would never have come out of the woods had my father-in-law not drove up."

Jackie didn't understand much about the law; neither did Jim or Steph or Larry, but they did understand the truth. What was keeping them in a constant state of horror was the manner in which Pitt blatantly disregarded the truth. They had the 911 calls on tape! The court had heard them. How could she accuse him of not making the calls?! Yet, as she plowed on, delicate yet determined, day after day, they could see the jury and spectators following her, listening. She seemed to be telling them, "Don't believe your lying eyes." And they appeared to be buying it. Reason and logic and truth seemed no longer to be factors. The nightmare enveloped Jason and his family; swallowed them.

"Deputy Book told you not to confront these people, didn't he, Mr. Veitch?"

"No, ma'am, he did not. Deputy Book told me that the only way that I was going to catch these people was to catch them myself."

Pitt moved in and stared directly into Jason's eyes; her head cocked curiously and her smile dangerous. "So when Deputy Book testified that he told you not confront these people, he wasn't telling the truth?"

"Yes, ma'am," Jason replied steadily, "that is correct."

"So you are saying he lied?!"

"Yes. He lied."

Jason was clearly rattled. But he was not going to be deterred. Jackie's eyes showed love and deep pride in her son. He told the truth.

Pitt strode to the evidence table, which lay before the jury box. She rested her hand lightly on the table and looked directly at the jury. "But the truth of the matter, Mr. Veitch, you went out there to catch somebody, didn't you?"

"No, ma'am. That's not true. I went out there to watch and to wait and to call the police. And that's exactly what I did."

Stephanie held Billy's arm. She was mentally urging Jason to stay the course and not allow Pitt to break him. If it was possible to support someone through sheer will power, then Steph intended to do it. She focused on Jason and gripped her daddy's arm tighter.

"No intention of approaching them," Pitt continued, her back still to Jason, "confronting them, doing a citizen's arrest, shooting them?"

"No, ma'am."

"Then why, Mr. Veitch, did you bring this?" In one swift movement, Pitt had hoisted the shotgun with her tiny hands and held it high over her head. There was an audible gasp from the spectators, as Pitt wheeled on Jason, revealing the weapon.

Jason flinched, but kept his voice calm. "I didn't know what would happen if I was discovered. I just wanted to be prepared and protect myself."

Pitt lay the gun back on the table, and began moving slowly toward Jason. "Mr. Veitch, you testified that you came out of the woods because you feared for your father-in-law's safety."

"Yes, ma'am, that's correct."

"He was safe enough at home in his bed, wasn't he?"

Jason paused and ducked his head. "Yes, ma'am."

"So you caused him to be there."

"Yes, ma'am."

"So you caused him to be in harm's way. It's you who created the danger, Mr. Veitch."

"Ms. Pitt," Jason spoke firmly, "I wasn't the only one there."

Stephanie smiled and Ellis covered a small grin with his hand. Jason's honest clarity seemed to finally create a crack in Pitt's demeanor. She adjusted her stance and began spitting out sentences with machine-gun fury.

"Mr. Veitch, do you understand that you are here because the Grand Jury of this county has indicted you on five counts; felony murder, three counts of aggravated assault, and possession of a firearm during the commission of a felony; you understand that, don't you?"

"I understand that."

"You are charged with unlawfully killing a young man, you understand that?"

"I understand the charges."

Pitt's hands were balled into fists. "What was his name?"

"Mr. Reymundo."

"What was his *full* name?"

"Juan Carlos Reymundo," Jason answered, his voice breaking.

"You understand that in Count 1 you are charged with causing the death of Juan Carlos Reymundo?"

"Yes, ma'am, I--"

"So, you admit you killed him!"

"No, I, no, " Jason was trembling and confused. His voice was cracking and his mind could not seem to keep up with Pitt's questions. "No, I did not admit I killed a man. I accidentally shot a man."

"You killed this man, didn't you, Mr. Veitch?!"

Jason noticed that Pitt's peachy makeup only covered to her jaw line and her neck was deep red. Veins stood out on her face.

"Ms. Pitt, I did not mean to kill Mr. Reymundo."

"Answer my question, sir," she demanded furiously, "you killed this man, didn't you?!"

Feeling a deep thickness in his face and throat, tears began to course down Jason's face, as he admitted, "Yes, ma'am, he is dead because of me."

"And he is dead because you shot him with a shotgun!"

"I poked Mr. Reymundo with a shotgun and the gun went off."

"You killed Juan Carlos Reymundo with this shotgun, didn't you?!"

"I accidentally killed him with that gun, yes, ma'am."

"Nobody else put this shotgun to his back, did they?"

"No, ma'am," Jason sobbed, "they did not."

"And you pulled the trigger."

"Mr. Reymundo was getting up." Jason's voice was suddenly forceful. "I thought he was going to pull a gun or a knife. I was scared to death. But this I know for sure, Ms. Pitt: I did not pick up that gun, aim it at Mr. Reymundo, put that gun on my shoulder and pull that trigger. No, ma'am, I did not do that."

If this moment gave Jason's family some hope, Pitt's icy calm took that hope away. No matter what Jason did or said, it appeared to fit right into Pitt's plans.

"So the fatal shot, the shot that killed him," Pitt spoke conversationally now, " was after you kicked him, wasn't it?"

"I did not kick Mr. Reymundo. I used my foot to push him back down."

Pitt wheeled toward Jason. "You pushed him to the ground with your foot?"

"Yes, yes, ma'am, that is correct," Jason stammered, unsure of her seeming delight at his answer.

"And why did you omit that from your direct testimony?"

"Wha-what direct testimony?"

"The direct testimony we just had a few minutes ago. You didn't say a word about that."

"But...Mr. Kane didn't ask me about that." Jason was truly baffled.

"So you lied to this court, didn't you, Mr. Veitch?"

"When? No, I...."

"Well, which is it, Mr. Veitch? Did you kick him or did you lie to this court?"

"I...I just...I don't..."

Jackie leaned forward and gazed at Mitchell Kane. She was hoping he would put a stop to this. But he sat, expressionless, and did not move.

"When you killed Mr. Reymundo, he was in a prone position, right?" I believe you called it a push-up position?"

"Ms. Pitt, I want to clarify that the gun did accidentally go off."

"Mr. Veitch, when you killed Juan Carlos Reymundo, his hands were in plain view, weren't they?"

Suddenly Kane was on his feet. "Your Honor, I object to the form of the question. He's answered the business about being killed; I ask her to....."

Somewhat relieved that this relentless hammering had been interrupted, Jackie turned her head away. Her gaze drifted toward the jury box. Each juror was listening carefully to Kane's objections and the judge's admonitions. Except for one. The stern juror on the front row was looking directly at Jackie, unblinking. His face, cold and hard, had a new expression. Lips curled almost into a grimace, he just stared at Jackie, eyes fixed. Jackie tried to hold his gaze and challenge him, but found she could not. She gripped her Bible hard and realized her hands were cold.

Pitt had returned to questioning Jason. "And you also failed to mention it when you talked to the police officer who showed up on the scene."

"On the night of the shooting?" Jason asked her.

"Allow me to say this in a way you can understand. You didn't mention all the details to the officer who showed up at the scene of the shooting, did you?"

"We didn't go into all the specific details at that time. I just answered the questions he asked me."

"You mean you just told him what you wanted him to know, right?"

"No, ma'am. I just told him that I accidentally shot the man. That was the most important thing to me, is that I accidentally shot a man."

"Because that's what you wanted him to hear from you, right?"

"Because that's the truth."

Stephanie found herself urging Jackie to eat some lunch, then realized she had not touched her own plate. Debbie, Cynthia, and Cynthia's husband had joined Larry, Jim, Billy, Stephanie, and Jackie for their mid-day meal. The only thing which seemed to be on everyone's mind, was the coming afternoon, and what it might bring.

As the court re-assembled, Jackie watched the jurors enter. Noticing the disturbed, focused set of her face, Larry spoke. "Honey, what you looking at?"

"It's that juror," she answered, "the one I told you about. Larry. He really scares me."

"An innocent young man is dead." Evelyn Pitt began her closing arguments. "Juan Carlos Reymundo is dead, and the Defendant killed him; no question, he killed him.

We are here to determine if that's okay with you. If that's okay with you, the designated spokespersons for Crockett County. Not only just for the parties involved, but by the permanent record and through the media for all the world to hear what kind of justice we have in Crockett County.

We are here to determine the guilt or innocence of Jason Veitch. And you have heard his testimony.

Now his testimony was quite obviously well choreographed, well scripted, which begs the question of course, if we're here to tell the truth, why does it have to be choreographed? Why does it have to be scripted?

And the answer is obvious, because the truth hurts, and he needs to avoid the truth. The Defendant, who had an excuse for everything, takes responsibility for nothing.

You know the facts. You know the Defendant was angry. As much as he tried to minimize that, you know he was angry; he lost a lot of money. He chose to go out there. He chose to go out there with a loaded gun. And despite the fact that the law is on the way, and these guys aren't going anywhere, he cannot restrain himself from taking justice into his own hands. He became the aggressor. He fired a shot to scare the people, to intimidate them, to place them in reasonable apprehension of immediately receiving a violent injury. He pointed the gun at them for the same reason; forced them to lie on the ground, gun on them the whole time.

He allowed his anger to override his reason; to override his judgment. His obsession with catching anybody who would steal from him overrode what a reasonable person would do. What he did to these three men was aggravated assault. And what he did to Mr. Reymundo was felony murder.

Ladies and Gentlemen, you cannot go out and create a situation by your own conduct, and then claim: 'Oh, because of that situation, I was forced to do something bad to someone.' You can't put the forces in motion that create the danger and then claim the danger as your defense.

Juan Carlos Reymundo is dead, and Jason Veitch did it. And I ask you, I implore you to not lose sight of that reality as you deliberate."

So there it was. Pitt had explained to the jurors, in a reasonable and persuasive manner, why Jason Veitch should go to jail for thirty years. Unlike her cross-examination of Jason, there was no anger or conjecture. She had taken cold facts and used them to her advantage. Pitt had reached the jury on a very human level. At the end of her statements, many members of the Hispanic community and Reymundo's family and friends were weeping. It appeared, from their pained faces, that some of the jurors might join them.

Mitchell Kane stood, upon the judge's invitation, and walked to the jury box. Jackie thought him quite imposing, and much sharper with the witnesses than she had expected. But something was missing. Had she really seen him save her child? Jackie felt empty and lost. Her faith seemed to be hovering some distance away. Kane began, quietly.

"On a dark Georgia night in February of 2008, two lives were accidentally destroyed. You cannot return Juan Carlos Reymundo to his family. You cannot return Jason Veitch to the life he knew before this tragic accident. But you can send Jason home.

Jason went out to his property on the evening of February 29 to help the police catch whoever was stealing from his property. He had tried everything else. He put up a sign that said, 'Smile, you're on camera.' He placed a vehicle on the site, hoping the burglars would think it was occupied. He made a police report every single time his houses got hit, and he got hit seventeen times. Seventeen times. He filed reports; he asked what could be done. And a young sheriff's deputy, with a long history of poor conduct and unprofessional behavior, flippantly gave him bad advice. Jason went out there, not because he was a vigilante or a Rambo, as the State wants you to believe, but because he was rightfully protecting his property, and he reacted to the situation which transpired because he was, quite simply, scared to death.

There's a law in this state called the Stand-Your-Ground Law. It used to be that even if you were in your home and somebody broke in there with a gun, you still had a duty to retreat. But no more. The Georgia Legislature has said that you don't have to retreat. You can stand your ground. And that's what Jason did. He stood his ground. It seems to me that the law was never designed to give you protection on the one hand, and to take it away with the other. The law was never designed to allow you to defend yourself, but if you do, defending yourself is a crime.

Now the Prosecutor would have you believe that these acts were committed by an enraged man who 'just wanted to shoot someone.' I want you to see Jason Veitch for who he is. He's a good man--" And then something extraordinary happened. Mitchell Kane burst into tears. He never lost his commitment to his closing words. And the emotion seemed to ambush him; in no way did it appear calculated. In fact, it was just a display of pure spontaneous emotion; nothing more or less. Kane caught himself, gained control of his voice, and with tears streaming down his face, continued, "-- a good man who was put in an impossible situation and did the best he could do. He's a good man.

Though he never intended harm, he knows a man died as a result of what he did. He knows that, every time he looks in the mirror. He knows that, every time he looks at his seven-year-old son; his son, who he's got to teach right from wrong. He will never get over that."

Kane gave the jury, the spectators, and the families one final look, then walked to his seat and sat down beside Jason. He never even saw the grateful smile on Jackie's face.

Judge Carroll spoke up. "The State has an opportunity to close closing arguments. Does the State wish to proceed?"

Pitt stood. "Please, Your Honor."

"You may do so."

A deputy brought in a large photograph mounted on an easel. This was Juan Carlos, smiling and wearing a crisp tuxedo. He was probably headed to his senior prom. Pitt stood still, just in front of it, and spoke softly and earnestly.

"May it please the Court and Counsel. Ladies and Gentlemen. I'm not going to take too long.

A young man is dead and it was all so unnecessary. His family mourns his loss, and this man did it. What he did went beyond what is legal and beyond what is justifiable. He set in motion the events that led to it; then he did it.

The Defendant is accountable for his conduct. He may not take responsibility for his actions, but he is accountable for the senseless devastation he has caused.

Juan Carlos Reymundo can no longer speak for himself. Jason Veitch saw to that. Juan Carlos can no longer ask for justice for himself and his grieving family. So I ask for him. Right here, right now, let's show the world what Georgia Justice means. You are duty bound to apply the law here. It's more than that; you have a sworn obligation to Juan Carlos, an oath that you made to God."

J.J. knelt beside his bed, saying his goodnight prayers. Stephanie and Jason sat on his bed, listening.

"...God, don't forget to bless Bojangles and my teacher. And please don't make me to go to school tomorrow. Amen."

As he climbed into bed, Stephanie tucked J.J.'s covers around him and asked him, "J.J., Honey, why don't you want to go to school tomorrow?"

J.J. studied his mother's face a moment before answering, "Will Daddy pick me up after school?"

Sitting on the edge of her son's bed, Steph chose her words very carefully. Jason stood and listened. "Probably. Maybe. We might be getting some big news for Daddy tomorrow and we...tomorrow is a big day."

J.J. turned and gazed directly at his daddy. "Will you pick me up after school tomorrow?" When no answer came, he spoke to Stephanie, "Mom, me and Daddy need to talk."

Holding back emotion, Stephanie did the last thing in the world that she wanted to do at this moment: stood, and left her two boys alone.

Jason placed one knee on the bed, then sat on the edge, reaching to smooth his boy's hair. "What you want to talk about, Big Man?"

"They're going to tell you about jail tomorrow."

Jason swallowed hard and fought to keep his voice steady. "Yes. We think tomorrow will be the day we find out."

"Are you scared?"

Jason nodded affirmatively and mustered up a conspiratorial smile for his son. "Are you?" he asked.

"Yes, sir, but not too much," said J.J. thoughtfully, "I talked to Jesus about it. And He told me that He goes to jail, too. So you won't ever be alone."

Beyond words now, Jason leaned forward and kissed J.J. on the forehead. He was crying and there was no use trying to hide. Starting to rise, Jason was stopped by J.J.'s voice.

"And there's something else I'm supposed to do. Just in case."

"And what is that?"

J.J. sat up in bed and gently grasped his daddy's face, one last time, between his little hands. Jason, understanding, took his boy's face between his own hands. And so they just sat there for a while. Making a memory. Looking at each other. Hard as they can.

CHAPTER ELEVEN

TRIAL - THE FINAL CLIMB

"WHY IS IT SO COLD IN THE COURTROOM TODAY?" JACKIE'S nose, hands, and feet felt heavy and frigid. The room was packed, and she thought that body heat alone would have warmed the space a bit. She couldn't remember getting dressed for court today, or why she had chosen such a drab outfit. Her hair, hanging limply about her face, was uncombed, and her unadorned lips were cracked and dry. Jackie's family looked so sad. The remaining faces filling the court were all strangers. She was aware of Larry squeezing her hand to the point that it was hurting. Jason stood in front of her, between Ellis and Kane, looking so helpless. And suddenly, the gavel came down, hard, and the judge pronounced the sentence. This was it? After all this time and all the pain, it came down to these few seconds? "Thirty years" and "federal penitentiary" spoken aloud and their lives were ended. People were screaming and chaos erupted all about Jason and his family. Flashbulbs blinded Jackie, and when she found her sight once again Stephanie had her arms around Jason and was refusing to let the guards put the cuffs back on him. Held firmly in Larry's grip, Jackie could only watch as deputies pulled Stephanie, crying and fighting, out of the room. And then, turning back to the little table at the front of the courtroom, she could see only Ellis and Kane, both motionless, their backs to her. No Jason. Gone already. Gone.

J.J. would not stop crying. He seemed to have lost all reason and would only cry for his daddy. Jackie couldn't recall where they had taken his mommy, but remembered that Stephanie had been heavily sedated. The house was dim and no one was about. Where was Larry? Why was no one helping her? She could not get J.J. to stop crying. He was hysterical and howled and gasped for breath between sobs. "Oh, God, please help us!" Jackie suddenly realized why the lights were so dark in the house. She couldn't breathe. She was starved for oxygen and her eyes were beginning to dim. If she passed out, or worse, what would happen to J.J.? Why was she alone? Why wasn't anyone helping her? Jackie lay down on the bed beside J.J. and dialed 911. When she heard, "911, What is your emergency?" Jackie could only rasp, "He won't stop crying, and I can't breathe." And then, the operator must have hung up on her, because the only sound she could hear was the dial tone, and J.J. crying.

Jackie looked at the phone in her hand, but did not remember picking it up. She could hear the dial tone, and from somewhere in the room, crying. Jackie spotted Bojangles, his tail tucked between his legs, whining in the corner of the room. Putting the phone receiver back on the cradle, Jackie pulled herself out of bed. She must feed Bojangles. Besides, it was getting light outside. Time to get ready for court. They told her this would be the last day.

Wearing a deep violet suit with a lace bodice, Jackie was dressed for the day. She was seated at the kitchen bar, a stack of documents and papers before her. Her Bible was opened and she read one verse over and over. Psalm 91:5: *Thou shalt not be afraid for the terror by night, nor for the arrow that flieth by day.* Behind her, Larry straightened his tie in the reflection of the coffee maker, then poured a cup. He sat the cup, without a sound, beside Jackie's Bible, then returned to pour a shot for himself. Passing the bar, Larry paused, moved the cup in, and closed Jackie's fingers around it. Jackie lifted the cup to her lips, took a sip, and continued to read.

Jim Veitch and his family scurried about their kitchen with the silent precision of a drill team. As Jim arose from the table, Hannah removed his dishes. Anna Grace delivered a sack lunch to her dad, for the mid-day break in the trial. Little Patience struggled to reach her dad's plate and carried it to the sink. Jennifer straightened the handkerchief in Jim's pocket. Suddenly, all was still. One by one, Jim kissed his girls and silently left the house. His four girls just watched. Soon Jason and Stephanie would be dropping off J.J.

Closing Stephanie's car door and crossing in front of the vehicle, Jason slid into the driver's seat. They would drop J.J. off with Jennifer, as they had so many days before, and Jen would take him to school, return to home-school her girls, then pick up J.J. at the end of the school day. They had been through this routine before, but probably would not experience it again. The car doors were shut and all seat belts were on, but the engine was not started. Jason gazed out the window.

"Daddy."

"Yes, J.J."

"I'll be late for school."

"All right, then."

Still, the engine did not crank and Jason did not move.

"Daddy."

"Yes, J.J."

"Don't be scared of the court today. We been praying for rainbows."

Jason turned the key and the engine came to life. The car backed out of the driveway and disappeared down the street.

At her request, the others had left Jackie alone during the lunch break. The morning had taken its toll. As grueling as the testimony and court proceedings were, the waiting was so much worse. Yet she could not leave this room. What if they came back with a verdict and she was out? A few stragglers milled about the court-room and chatted, but she sat, a solitary figure, by herself on the long bench.

Debbie entered the back of the courtroom, padded silently down the aisle, taking a seat beside her cousin.

"You eat any lunch?" Jackie did not seem to hear or notice Debbie's arrival. "I got a breakfast bar in my purse somewhere..."

"One way or another," Jackie half-whispered, "we're gonna find out today."

"Will you eat it if I find it?"

"Kane says there's no way those twelve jurors could agree on all those charges."

"Why don't we get up and walk around, Jackie?"

"He doesn't think Jason will be coming home with us today."

"Get some air."

"You know what Kane said when Jason decided on the jury trial? He said, 'You have made a huge mistake.'"

Every so gently, Debbie helped Jackie to her feet.

"Come on, cuz; let's go see if the sky's cleared up any."

When Debbie had finished helping Jackie down the concrete steps, she searched the sky for a break in the clouds. Turning, she spied Jackie with one hand on her Bible, the other on the steps, and she was lowering herself to the ground. Jackie then sank to her knees, placed her Bible on the steps, and bent her head forward. The steps would be her altar and her prayer closet. At the top of the stairs, two cameramen who were propped against the building smirked at Jackie and began snapping pictures.

"Jackie? Honey, don't..."

Jackie did not turn to face her cousin, but spoke with conviction. "Twelve people are back there deciding what will happen to my son. What can I do? I'm gonna pray for him, and for them, and for us. Right here. Debbie, you can join me or leave me."

Debbie eyed her cousin, on her knees before the world, then looked up at the men staring down at them. Deliberately, Debbie sank down and clasped her hands, giving the men one more bold look before she bowed her head.

Jackie prayed. "Dear Lord, help us now. We understand You have the answers and know what we must face this day. But my poor, weak, human side is afraid. And so I come to You as a child. And I listen. Whatever is being decided in that room right now, take care of my child. Take care of my little Bird and give him protection under Your wings... " Then her voice broke. There was nothing left.

A soft breeze picked up Jackie's hair and swept it across her face. She didn't feel it. She only felt soft, submissive, willing.

"For He shall give His angels charge over thee, to keep thee in all thy ways." The words came from behind her. Jim had silently appeared, along with Cynthia and several others, and he picked up

137

his mom's prayer, when she could not finish. "Thank you, Lord, for Your protection throughout the dark night, and for the joy that comes in the morning. Thank You for the faith to walk through the valley of the shadow and fear no evil. Thank You for helping our brother...for helping my brother..."

Jim had grown silent and lifted his head to the top of the stairs. Sensing this, both Debbie and Jackie raised their eyes upward. Standing before the massive copper doors stood Ellis and Mitchell Kane.

"It's time."

It was so cold in the courtroom. Jason was in front of her, looking small and helpless. Jackie could not help but notice the similarities between this moment and her nightmares. As terrible as they were, she was hoping this was one of the daymare/nightmare/dreams she had experienced. But it was real. This was really happening.

Judge Carroll addressed the packed, silent courtroom.

"Ladies and Gentlemen, let me remind you that this is a matter that requires utmost dignity. As I said before, a young man has perished and another's life is in the balance. There will be no cause for outward disagreement or celebration no matter what this verdict is. Has the jury reached a verdict?"

And the juror with the black eyes, the one who had frightened Jackie so with his icy stares, rose and said simply, "We have, Your Honor."

"Oh, please, Lord. Not him," Jackie thought to herself. Larry turned to her and Jackie realized she had spoken aloud.

In even tones, the judge instructed, "Please hand the verdict form to the bailiff."

Jackie was aware that Stephanie had averted her eyes and was clutching Jim's hand and her father's hand. She could feel Larry's hand on her arm; her free hand clutched her Bible. The verdict was passed from the juror to the bailiff, from the bailiff to the deputy, from the deputy to the judge, but the bearers seem to disappear. Jackie could only see the white paper, moving in slow motion across the courtroom and up to the judge's lofty station. And then the judge opened the pages and read silently. Jackie scanned Judge Carroll's face for any reaction when she finally put the verdict down, looked out across the courtroom, and spoke.

"Will the Defendant please rise?"

Jason stood. Ellis stood on his left. Kane stood on his right. Stephanie, hand still clutched in Jim's hand, leaned into her father. Larry placed his hand protectively around Jackie's head and drew her close. Jason's head suddenly jerked back and his knees buckled. Both Ellis and Kane grabbed Jason's hands and helped him recover and remain on his feet. And then, Judge Carroll began to read.

"The State of Georgia versus Jason Richard Veitch. We, the jury, find the Defendant..."

Jennifer pulled into a parking space and checked her watch. School would be out in about two minutes; she would go to the front steps to wait for J.J.

"Girls, stay in the car. I'll get J.J. and be right back."

Hannah nodded and smiled. Jennifer knew her eldest would lock the car doors and carefully supervise Anna Grace and Patience until she returned with their cousin.

Walking down the long brick trail to the front entrance, Jennifer noted what a beautiful building this was, with its stonework, high windows and lush landscaping. And it had become a beautiful day too, with the morning clouds burning off. Still she felt no joy. Then her phone buzzed. Text message. It was Jim. Her heart jumped into her hand and she dropped the phone in the grass. Hurriedly retrieving it, Jennifer locked her eyes on the message: Verdict In --

Jennifer ran down the hall of J.J.'s school, searching for his classroom. When she burst through the door, Miss Inez turned sternly toward the intrusion and the children flinched and reacted with startled looks. "It's in," Jennifer gasped. "The verdict in is. J.J.'s daddy."

It seemed as if time stopped. The words, "We, the jury, find the Defendant....," hung in the air for the eternity that passes between two heartbeats. Then the judge's voice continued.

"-- not guilty of felony murder. One B, we the jury find the Defendant not guilty of involuntary manslaughter as a result of pointing a gun. C, we the jury find the Defendant not guilty of involuntary manslaughter as a result of reckless conduct. D, we the jury find the Defendant not guilty as a result of simple battery. E, we the jury find the Defendant not guilty of involuntary manslaughter during the commission of a lawful act. So says the jury. Ladies and Gentlemen, it's been a long journey. Let's go home."

Stephanie had reached over the back of the bench and pulled Jason, backwards, to her. Awkwardly, she held him from behind, almost in a stranglehold, and would not let go. Jackie could only lift her hands heavenward and say, "Thank You, Thank You, Thank You...." She could not seem to stop saying it, nor did she want to. All over the courtroom, mixing with the sobs and cries, hands were raised heavenward, some waving about, some waving pages from the Bible. It was a quiet revival in a Georgia courtroom. And one family got to go home again.

Outside the courtroom, the spectators and films crews emptied into a new spring day. The first hint of green was glowing and branches were lifted by a soft afternoon breeze. Pitt had apparently made a quick getaway, for she and Crutcher were nowhere to be seen on the front steps. Kane was speaking to a reporter as Jackie and Larry skirted past him. Jason and Stephanie burst through the doors and just stood at the top of the stairs, flanked by two deputies. Jason looked at the sky with new eyes. People passed, looked, but gave them their space.

Suddenly Stephanie's attention was drawn to a lone figure descending the steps. She squeezed Jason's hand and broke away. "Mister," she called, taking the steps two at a time, "Mister!" Slowly the lone man turned, a stern look on his face. The Foreperson with the cold eyes just stared at Stephanie as she approached him. Stephanie opened her mouth to speak, but her lips worked soundlessly. Her body and arms moved helplessly, as she tried to express thanks, but words did not come. The Foreperson just stared for a moment, and then his face contorted and twisted. With a muffled gasp, he drew his hand to his mouth and broke into a sobbing spasm. Stephanie lurched toward him, armed outstretched. He reached toward Steph with both arms and they hugged one another, lost in tears and wordless expression of emotion. He held her like a lost child. One of the other jurors watched for a moment, then gently moved in and placed her hand on Stephanie's back. Debbie moved to the Foreperson and slid her arm around his waist, leaning her head against him. And so it went, one by one, jurors, family, observers, all moved together and held, smiling, talking, crying, and hugging in the warm sunshine.

Jason still stood at the top of the stairs; alone. Drawing her eyes away from the group on the landing, Jackie, her Bible held firmly, looked up at her son. Teasing gusts nudged at his collar and lifted a lock of hair. He was, for a moment, just a boy. Their eyes met. For the first time in forever, there was no need to rush. They moved toward one another easily, and met near the members of the flock, who were still laughing and crying and talking and touching. Jackie and Jason extended their arms, taking each other's hands. Jason opened his right hand, and something fell onto Jackie's left palm. It was the page that she tore from the Bible for him. She opened her hand, and her crumpled page fell into his hand. They held hands for a moment, with the verses of Psalms between them.

Suddenly J.J. was leaping out of Jennifer's van and bounding up the steps into his daddy's arms. They hugged and hugged until Bojangles made his way to them and began to jump and yip for attention. And then they hugged Bo.

Jackie turned and watched a little group walking across the grass toward the road. It was Mrs. Reymundo, being helped to her car. Without a pause, Jackie crossed the lawn, calling her name, and finally catching her attention.

Jason watched as his mother and the mother of the man he had killed spoke. At one point Mrs. Reymundo held out her son's photograph, showed it to Jackie, and spoke intensely to her. Then she was ushered away, and Jackie turned back to join her family. What the two mothers said, what passed between them, would never be known.

As she walked easily back to her family, Jackie reflected back on the last ten months. Is that how long it had been since the night of that terrible phone call? Yes, three hundred days of darkness.

And while Jason was locked in that cell, nine days of black night. Jackie looked up at the blue sky and white clouds. So real they seemed unreal. And the red brick building across the road caught her eye. She had seen it every day of the trial, but had never looked up. There, high atop the building was a steeple, and on the steeple, her beloved cross rose heavenward to the bright sky. A church. Funny, she had never known that they had been in the shadow of the cross every day. All she had to do, was look up.

EPILOGUE

THE HOUSE BLOOMED FROM THE GEORGIA SOIL AND NESTLED ON the side of a hill, and looked down on her mama and daddy's house.

Larry had taken Jackie out to the house, still not quite completed, during the trial. She walked through those beautiful front doors and saw, dancing with sunlight, the Roman style pool that was the interior centerpiece of the house. She saw her girlhood dream house before her. She had so much. And yet, it meant nothing without her Jason. "If someone walked through that door and told me they could bring Jason back," she promised God, "I'd give them this house; I'd give them everything." And yet He had not asked for anything in return, other than her faith.

Before the verdict was announced, Jackie had shouted silently, "Mountain, crumble and fall!" And her faith, having been shattered and then rebuilt to the size of a mustard seed, was enough. It was enough. Indeed, the mountain crumbled to dust, and God blew it away.

Jackie sat on her veranda, enjoying this warm, breezy morning. From her vantage point, she could see movement in her parents' kitchen, just down the hill. What a gift to have family so near. A gift among many.

Later in the week she would travel to another state, to speak about her family, the trial, her faith. When asked if she was ever nervous speaking to such large crowds, she would always answer the same, "I was nervous when I went into cell block A to see my son in jail. I was frightened when my doctor told me I was a dead woman walking, and rushed me to the hospital. I was scared when the jury came in and the judge asked, 'Have you reached a verdict?' But am I nervous tonight?" she'd shout with a glorious smile. And then, practically vibrating and levitating with joy and energy, "No, I'm not nervous; not even close. Because I have claimed my miracle and I am living under the shadow of His wings!"

Jackie Carpenter is a tiny woman. But even on the largest of stages, she is a force of nature, an emissary of God, and a missionary for His Message. She speaks from her heart, so it reaches to the hearts of others.

But today, she is just a little Georgia girl, sitting in her dream house, surrounded by her dogs and enjoying the first daffodils of spring.

Maybe tomorrow, though, she will do something different. Maybe she'll host a movie night for her beloved grandchildren. Or perhaps she'll swim in her pool with moonlight shining on her through the towering windows. Or maybe she'll do something really adventurous. Who knows? No mountain is too high.

A WORD FROM AUTHOR MICHAEL MCCLENDON

ASK JACKIE CARPENTER HOW SHE IS TODAY, AND SHE WILL TELL you: "I still go to Faith Rehab on an outpatient basis at least seven times per week. Should another tragedy strike, God has promised that my Room #91 in His Hospital of Psalms has an opening any time. I have the best insurance plan in the world; my debt was paid in full by God's son. Any time I need to be re-admitted, He will welcome me with open arms and his Shield of Protection will safeguard me from man and the world."

Jackie gives me hope.

I share an odd little incident that will help describe Jackie and her heart, which is as big as her faith.

On the first night of filming the motion picture version of Jackie's story, we were shooting on location in the forest. Temps in the 20's were predicted, but instead we got a tornado that was heralded by hours of miserable rain. The actors portraying Reymundo, Morales, and Lerma, had been face down in icy, slick Georgia clay for hours. Their clothing was so heavy with mud that they had trouble rising from their prone positions. We were soaked and chilled to the bone. And about 3am, in the midst of this misery, comes Jackie. Now Miz Jackie lights up a room, even in sweats. But she walked into those woods in a gorgeous tailored suit, high heels, hair and makeup perfect, and a pastel umbrella keeping her in pristine condition. She lit the night. Jackie watched from the side; we finally called it a wrap. The tornado was to hit us within minutes, destroying some of the equipment. The actors stood, packed with mud and dripping with rain and slush, and prepared to tramp back to their trailers. Jackie closed her umbrella and put it aside. Then she strode through the mud in her heels, rain assaulting her pale suit, and gathered these three muddy actors in her arms, hugging and holding them.

This is Jackie. She's a ray of beauty, style, and light on a dark night. And she's a warm hug when you are tired and cold.

It's an honor to know and love Jackie Carpenter. I highly recommend it.

CPSIA information can be obtained
at www.ICGtesting.com
Printed in the USA
LVHW03s1218200818
587501LV00009B/526/P